Mental Health Needs of Children and Young People with Intellectual Disabilities

A reader for professionals and support staff in health, education and social care

2nd Edition

Foreword by
Professor Sheila the Baroness Hollins

Edited by Dr Sarah H Bernard & Dr Jane McCarthy

Mental Health Needs of Children and Young People with Intellectual Disabilities

A reader for professionals and support staff in health, education and social care

© Pavilion Publishing & Media

The authors have asserted their rights in accordance with the Copyright, Designs and Patents Act (1988) to be identified as the authors of this work.

Published by:
Pavilion Publishing and Media Ltd
Blue Sky Offices, 25 Cecil Pashley Way
Shoreham by Sea, West Sussex
BN43 5FF

Tel: 01273 434 943
Email: info@pavpub.com
Web: www.pavpub.com

Published 2020

A catalogue record for this book is available from the British Library.

ISBN: 978-1-912755-49-3

Pavilion Publishing and Media is a leading publisher of books, training materials and digital content in mental health, social care and allied fields. Pavilion and its imprints offer must-have knowledge and innovative learning solutions underpinned by sound research and professional values.

Editors: Dr Sarah H Bernard & Jane McCarthy
Production editor: Mike Benge, Pavilion Publishing and Media Ltd
Cover design: Emma Dawe, Pavilion Publishing and Media Ltd
Page layout and typesetting: Emma Dawe, Pavilion Publishing and Media Ltd
Printing: Ashford Press

Contents

Acknowledgements

This is the second edition of the book, originally entitled 'Mental Health Needs of Children and Young People with Learning Disabilities' (2010) and edited by Raghu Raghavan, Dr Sarah H Bernard and Jane McCarthy.

We wish to thank all the children and young people with intellectual disabilities, their families, carers and professionals who have helped us to conceptualise the theme of this book through our practice and research. We wish to acknowledge the help and support of all the chapter contributors to this book. We are grateful to Jan Alcoe from Pavilion Publishing for commissioning this book and for her support and patience.

Contributors

Dr Ruksana Ahmed is a Consultant Clinical Psychologist with the Centre for Interventional Paediatric Psychopharmacology and Rare Diseases (CIPPRD) in National and Specialist CAMHS at South London and Maudsley NHS Foundation Trust. Dr Ahmed's areas of clinical expertise include working with children and young people with intellectual disabilities and neurodevelopmental conditions and co-occurring mental health problems in the context of chronic health conditions and rare diseases. Dr Ahmed also provides highly specialist supervision, training and consultation to multi-disciplinary and multi-agency professionals and teams across the UK. Dr Ahmed has held several clinical and lead posts within Child and Adolescent Mental Health Services (CAMHS) in London and in the United Arab Emirates (UAE). These roles have included Psychological Therapies Lead within CAMHS in East London NHS Foundation Trust and CAMHS Lead Psychologist – Maudsley Health, UAE. In addition to Dr Ahmed's clinical experience her leadership and strategic experience has included lead roles within the transformation of CAMHS community services for children with a range of mental health conditions and intellectual disabilities across East London. Dr Ahmed is an Honorary Consultant Clinical Psychologist at Great Ormond Street Hospital NHS Trust and is also an Honorary Lecturer within the Research Department of Clinical, Educational and Health Psychology at University College London. Dr Ahmed is also an Associate Fellow of the British Psychological Society.

Tina Bang-Andersen is a specialist lead occupational therapist with CAMHS Neuropsychiatry and Challenging Behaviour Team, Service for Complex Autism and Associated Neurodevelopmental Disorders (SCAAND) and director at SensoryLiving. Tina qualified in 1999 from the School of Occupational Therapy in Copenhagen, Denmark, and has worked in England since qualification. She has worked for a number of years in adult mental health, acute, forensic and community settings. Tina started specialising in intellectual disability and autism in 2006 and has worked within this field since. She specialises in occupational coaching, sensory integration and primitive reflexes. She focuses on the needs of the child and how they can be met within the context of family life, school environment and the community. She is also skilled in delivering teaching and training for families, school staff and other professionals.

Dr Sarah H Bernard has been a Consultant Psychiatrist in child intellectually disability for over 25 years. She leads a national/specialist multidisciplinary outpatient service offering assessment and intervention to children and young people with ID. Sarah has been involved with service development, teaching and training and research at a national level. She has worked with the Royal College of Psychiatrists, NHS England, third sector and voluntary organisations, social care and education. She is Trust named doctor for child safeguarding and clinical director of the CAMHS - South London Partnership.

Stephanie Carr, MSc., is a Clinical Specialist Speech and Language Therapist and Positive Behavioural Support Lead for Teesside CAMHS. Stephanie is a clinician in Teesside CAMHS, where her day-to-day role involves supporting young people with a range of behavioural differences throughout the service.

Eddie Chaplin is Professor of Mental Health in Neurodevelopmental Disorders at London South Bank University. He has extensive clinical experience in local and national mental health services for people with neurodevelopmental conditions and has also developed a number of post graduate courses relating to offending and the mental health of people with NC. His research interests include neurodevelopmental conditions and offending and evaluating coproduced mental health promotion strategies and he developed the first guided self-help manual specifically aimed at people with intellectual disability. Eddie has an extensive publication portfolio and is Editor for the Advances in Autism.

Dr Alison Dunkerley is a Consultant who works in generic CAMHS (Child and Adolescent Mental Health Services) and has a special interest in children with ID (Intellectual Disability). She presently works in Central Manchester. She is dual trained in CAMHS and Psychiatry of ID and has worked as a consultant within this speciality for 17 years. She has also worked in other CAMHS within the North-West region of England. She has contributed to other publications including the 1st edition of this book and is involved in research projects with this population including the present trial investigating the effectiveness of bumetanide in the autism population. Presently, she sits on the executive committee for the faculty of ID within the Royal College of Psychiatrists. Working with this population has been both challenging and rewarding, particularly working with colleagues from other disciplines and she hopes to continue to contribute to the ongoing literature and research within this area.

Dr Suzannah Gratton, BSc (Hons), MSc, PsychD, CPsychol, has worked as a clinical psychologist with young people with intellectual disability and their families for most of the last 16 years. She has worked in local and national services offering assessment and intervention with particular interests in issues such as adapting CBT approaches to be suitable for young people with intellectual disability, assessment of capacity and consent and the role of cognitive assessments in understanding strengths and challenges. Suzannah enjoys providing supervision and supporting trainee clinical psychologists to develop skills in working with young people with intellectual disability through teaching and supervision.

Suzannah is currently the principal clinical psychologist in a local autism assessment service where she is working to redesign services to address issues of long waiting times and rising referral rates; she has also been facing the challenges of moving assessments online due to Covid-19.

Dr Heather Hanna FRCPsych is a Consultant Child and Adolescent Psychiatrist in Intellectual Disability. In 2018, she was the Royal College of Psychiatrist's UK 'Psychiatrist if the Year'. This award recognised Heather's work in establishing and leading Northern Ireland's first fully inclusive ID CAMH service. The service has been recognised for its innovation, outcomes and child-centred approaches. Heather leads on strategy and policy work at a regional and national level, particularly in relation to development of services for children and young people with intellectual disability and reduction of restrictive practices. She has particular interests in public health and co-production. Heather is founder and co-chair of a growing ID CAMHS clinical network across the island of Ireland.

Dr Kate Johnston, BSc, MSc, D Clin Psy, AFBPS, Consultant Clinical Psychologist, is a consultant clinical psychologist working in the Adolescent At-risk & Forensic Service, National & Specialist CAMHS. She has clinical and research interests in neurodevelopmental differences. She previously worked with adults with autism/ADHD in inpatient services and has undertaken research into neuropsychological functioning and adapting and evaluating psychological assessments and interventions for individuals with neurodevelopmental differences, including those involved in, or at risk of, youth offending.

Dr Martha Laxton-Kane, Consultant Clinical Psychologist, was brought up in Nottinghamshire by her parents with her two older siblings, Sara and Paul. Paul has severe ID and ASD and it is no coincidence that she has spent most of her career working with either young people or adults with ID and their families. Martha initially worked as a support worker at a residential school for ID and then as an Assistant Psychologist supporting the post-transition phase back into the community for many adults who had lived at the long stay hospital in Newark. When qualified she worked in a CAMHS team before going back to Newark again to work with adults with ID. From 2007 she then took up a post in her home town of Chesterfield to start up and lead an ID CAMHS team within Chesterfield Royal Hospital. Now she also manages the Child Development Psychology service at the same trust. Martha is currently a member of the committee for Children and Young People ID Psychology network and a member of the National LD Senate.

Karen Lewis has worked full-time as a Speech and Language Therapist since qualifying in 1987. Following working in a variety of community, hospital and educational settings, Karen was seconded for 6 months to a Regional

Communication Aid Centre which fired in her the desire to work with people with the most severe level of communication difficulties. When a post became available there in 1989, Karen secured this and so began her lifelong passion working with people in need of Augmentative and Alternative Communication (AAC). For the next 20 years she assessed people across the North of England until service re-organisation required her to be redeployed. She next joined Ferndene, a purpose-built inpatient service for Children and Young People with a range of complex difficulties and needs, including mental health and intellectual disabilities. She has worked at Ferndene for over ten happy years, bringing to this her previous AAC experience as well as learning and gaining experience in many new areas reflecting the diversity of the young people they serve. She also has a particular interest and lead role in local support for the Trust's agenda around reducing physical interventions and restrictive practice.

Dr Mark Lovell is a dual-trained Child and Adolescent Intellectual Disability Psychiatrist and Chief Clinical Information Officer based in Teesside, UK, working for Tees, Esk and Wear Valleys NHS Foundation Trust. He has worked with people with disabilities since his mid-teens from teaching outdoor pursuits, offering 24 hour care through to mental health and neurodevelopmental assessment and treatment. He chairs the Child and Adolescent Intellectual Disability Psychiatry Network internationally and has roles within the Royal College of Psychiatrists, British Academy of Childhood Disability and the Association for Child and Adolescent Mental Health. Mark has inputted into NHS England, NHS Digital, NHS X, Public Health England, Health Education England and Department for Education initiatives within his clinical interest areas of Child and Adolescent Intellectual Disabilities, Mental Health, Autism Spectrum Disorders and Informatics. He is a keen educator and author and has had involvement in the MindEd and DisabilityMatters educational websites.

Dr Jane McCarthy is Medical Lead for Learning Disability Service, Sussex Partnership NHS Foundation Trust, Honorary Associate Professor in Psychological Medicine, University of Auckland, New Zealand and Visiting Senior Lecturer, King's College London. Dr McCarthy has over 25 years of experience as a Consultant Psychiatrist working with people with intellectual disabilities. Dr. McCarthy's key research interests include the outcomes of psychiatric disorders in people with intellectual disabilities and she has significantly contributed to research in this area having obtained funding for a number of research initiatives including *'Assessment & early interventions for offenders with intellectual disabilities and autism'*. She is editor of the journal *Advances in Autism: International outcomes in education, health and care*. Dr McCarthy was Clinical Advisor on Adults with Autism for the Department of Health, England and Vice Chair of the Psychiatry of Intellectual Disability Faculty of Royal College of Psychiatrists.

Natasa Momcilovic BA, PGDip Child Art Psychotherapy, MSc, MBACP, is a clinical behaviour therapist with the Mental Health of Intellectual Disability Team which is a stream of the national and specialist CAMHS for complex autism and neuro developmental disorders (SCAAND) at the Maudsley Hospital. She leads a specialist Prader Willi Service that focuses on specialist assessments and management of mental health problems and challenging behaviours in young people with PWS. Her expertise is in working with children and adolescents with complex behaviour problems and family situations, and she has developed a psychoeducation programme for PWS. She is a trained course leader in Webster-Stratton parenting approach and has piloted a parenting programme based on the Webster-Stratton principles for parents of children with intellectual disability. Her particular interests include parenting approaches, challenging behaviours in Prader-Willi Syndrome and feeding problems in children with intellectual disability and autism. Natasa has undertaken research in treatment of challenging behaviours and published on that subject. She leads training events for charities and local organisations, presents on training events for other professionals and teaches on postgraduate programmes including psychiatrist trainees and a Doctorate in Clinical Psychology course at Kings College. Mrs Momcilovic completed Master's Degree in Special Education and Rehabilitation (1989) at the University of Zagreb, Croatia. She completed a Postgraduate Diploma in Child Art Psychotherapy (1995) and MSc in Mental Health Studies (1996) at the United Medical and Dental School of Guy's and St. Thomas's, London.

Dr Troy Tranah is a Consultant Clinical Psychologist, Head of the Adolescent At-risk & Forensic Service and Head of Psychology and Psychotherapy for Child & Adolescent Mental Health Services for the South London & Maudsley NHS Foundation Trust. He is also an Honorary Lecturer in Clinical Psychology at the Institute of Psychiatry, Psychology & Neuroscience, King's College London. As a Consultant Clinical Psychologist, he has developed a number of successful clinical services including Forensic, Childcare and Dialectical Behaviour Therapy services. Dr Tranah's current research interests include an evaluation of Dialectical Behaviour Therapy in the treatment of emerging borderline personality disorder, empathy and other factors associated with antisocial behaviour in adolescents and he is currently leading a treatment trial exploring a collaboration between the participatory arts and Dialectical Behaviour Therapy. Dr Tranah has published peer reviewed academic papers on a wide range of topics including, young offenders, self-harm, suicide, post-traumatic stress disorder and intellectual disabilities.

Foreword

It gives me great delight to provide the foreword for this book. The mental health of young people is high on the government's agenda, but we have ongoing work to do to ensure that it is better understood with respect to children and young people with intellectual disabilities. This book provides an evidence-based source of information that will be equally accessible to professionals and parents. As I write, we are living through the COVID-19 pandemic, which is taking the lives of the most disabled people in our society and will have long-term consequences for many more who are dependent on others for their daily needs and care. It reminds us of the importance of ensuring that we do not lose sight of the ongoing mental health needs of children and young people with intellectual disabilities, who are the most at risk of mental disorder. We have to ensure that this group of children and young people are not disadvantaged as they have every right to the same robust evidenced-based mental health care as their non-disabled peers.

In the UK there are approximately 286,000 children aged up to 17 years of age with an intellectual disability. Of these, as many as 40% are likely to develop mental health problems, often as a consequence of adverse childhood experiences. For many families, mental health problems and associated behaviours constitute a major challenge in accessing the right support, including access to mainstream education. A recent report from the Children's Commissioner titled Far Less than They Deserve published in May 2019 highlighted the experiences of children with intellectual disabilities and/or autism who have been placed in psychiatric institutions at some distance from their families despite evidence of poor or restrictive practices. Young people and their families need the best assessment and the right interventions at critical points to avoid hospital admission. For a very small number of young people, hospital admission might be in their best interests in order to offer safe and robust assessment of a complex mental health presentation. But such admissions must avoid retraumatising the person and must also provide their assessment in an environment which recognises any sensory or other individual needs if they are not to set up a vicious cycle of readmissions. Instead, admissions should be thought of as a 'last option' in a care pathway of skilled community assessment and interventions, and discharge should be anticipated at the earliest moment once the specialist assessment has been completed. It is essential that all professionals and their families are aware of the best approaches to challenge services on what is the safest and most effective intervention.

This book provides up-to-date evidence for the assessments, interventions and service developments that are needed to achieve better outcomes for children and young people with intellectual disabilities presenting with mental health needs, while also ensuring that any economic consequences of Covid-19 do not unequally disadvantage them.

Professor Sheila the Baroness Hollins
Emeritus Professor of Psychiatry of Intellectual Disability
Crossbench Peer, House of Lords, UK

References

Children's Commissioner (2019) Far Less than They Deserve. *Children with intellectual disabilities or autism living in mental health hospitals.* www.childrenscommissioner.gov.uk/wp-content/uploads/2019/05/CCO-far-less-than-they-deserve-2019.pdf

Section I:
Introduction, prevalence and legal issues

Chapter 1: Introduction

Jane McCarthy and Dr Sarah H Bernard

Chapter summary

This chapter is an introduction to the issues that children and young people with intellectual disabilities face in receiving the right support when presenting with mental health needs. We acknowledge the diversity of this group of young people and that professionals working in this field have used the available evidence in writing their chapters to address the day-to-day practice issues of assessment, treatment and care.

Background to the book

Worldwide, between 10% to 20% of children and adolescents experience mental disorder. It is reported that approximately a third of a million young people in the UK have intellectual disabilities and, of these, about 36% develop mental health problems (Emerson & Hatton, 2007). The nature and manifestation of mental health disorders in this population produces a complex and perplexing picture in terms of detection, diagnosis and therapeutic services.

With this in mind, this book aims to update the first edition, published nearly 10 years ago, to describe the ongoing issues relating to the care of children and young people with intellectual disabilities who present with mental health needs. We believe that through the consolidation of evidence-based practice for assessment, intervention and service provision, professionals will be able to provide high-quality and personalised care for young people with intellectual disabilities who have mental health needs. In the past 10 years, the main change seen in the field has been an increasing emphasis on understanding the diverse needs of this group, but also that services must develop in a way that keeps the young person within community settings nearer to families so that the most complex group do not spend many years in long-term hospital care or at a distance from their families. However, the main challenge to this area of practice, despite the first edition being written a decade ago, is that the current available evidence on interventions is limited, and what evidence we have is not specific to this group of young people. As professionals we therefore rely on the evidence generated from the wider population of young people (Veereenoogle *et al*, 2018).

We believe that family involvement and the enormous contribution made by parent support groups and organisations that strive to improve the understanding of the needs of these young people, and the excellent information they provide to both the young person, their families and professionals, is essential in the future delivery of good outcomes. We see this book as a significant contribution to this, bringing together the most up-to-date knowledge for the long-term benefit of children and young people with intellectual disabilities.

Our society is becoming more diverse and complex in terms of ethnicity, culture, language and gender identity. We have not devoted specific chapters to diversity because an awareness of the identity of each person should be embedded in all areas of a practice, and we asked authors to address any specific issues within their chapters. Currently, there is little evidence on how young people view their own identity, especially among those who have additional mental health needs. The experiences of children and young people with intellectual disabilities from minority ethnic communities and their families in accessing and using child and adolescent mental health services can at times be one of exclusion and discrimination. A number of factors, such as cultural and religious beliefs, language barriers, lack of adequate knowledge and awareness of services, act as barriers to accessing and using a range of services and professional help (Raghavan & Pawson, 2010).

Family carers of adults with intellectual disabilities from minority ethnic communities are more likely to report negative experiences of services, as well as negative relationships with local communities (Hatton *et al*, 2010). A systematic review that considered ethnic influences on the use of mental health services by people with intellectual disabilities found that South Asian children and adolescents in the UK had lower use of mental health services than a white British comparison group (Dura Villa & Hodes, 2012). A number of earlier studies in the US found that Latino mothers of young adults with intellectual disabilities were more at risk of poor well-being, were more socially disadvantaged, unemployed and unmarried, compared to mothers who described themselves as Anglo (Eisenhower & Blacher, 2006). In the UK, similar findings of increased psychological distress among South Asian carers of children and adolescents with intellectual disabilities was found to be mediated through socio-economic deprivation (Emerson *et al*, 2004).

There is a slowly growing evidence base around the experiences of people with intellectual disabilities who identify as lesbian, gay, bisexual and transgender (LGBT). Carers and services need to be aware of, and responsive to, the particular needs of this group (McCann *et al*, 2016). To date, most of the research has been exploratory or descriptive (Wilson *et al*, 2016). It is important to note that having intellectual disabilities should not add a further barrier to accessing support, as a person's cognitive ability may impact on how they express their gender identity.

Young people with intellectual disabilities who identify as LGBT may be the most invisible of all sexual minorities.

It is everyone's responsibility to keep children and young people safe, and it is crucial that all professionals and service providers are aware and have a good understanding of the identification of safeguarding issues. Children and young people with intellectual disabilities are known to be at an increased risk of abuse when compared with their non-disabled peers (Jones *et al*, 2012); thus all aspects of assessment, intervention and service planning must address and consider this within their structures. Increased risks arise because of communication difficulties, misunderstandings and inadequate assessments of behavioural disturbance. There may also be a lack of professional awareness of how all forms of abuse and neglect present in children and young people with intellectual disabilities (NSPCC, 2016). Certain behaviours risk being normalised as a result of the child's intellectual level. In addition, children and young people with disabilities are more likely to experience deprivation, thus compounding the situation. The young person's disability also increases the risk of their isolation from community networks, both for them and their family, resulting in safeguarding concerns being hidden and not reaching the attention of professionals.

A definition of safeguarding includes:

- Protecting children from maltreatment.
- Preventing impairment of children's health or development.
- Ensuring that children grow up in circumstances consistent with the provision of safe and effective care.
- Taking action to enable all children to have the best outcomes.

(DfE, 2018)

The Children Act (1989) provides extensive information regarding the safeguarding of children and young people and the legal frameworks to be considered.

It is beyond the scope of this book to adequately detail the extensive consideration of safeguarding referrals, assessment and legalities. Readers should access information from their local authority's safeguarding website if safeguarding concerns arise. There should be a low threshold for seeking expert advice in such cases.

The book's structure

Children and young people with intellectual disabilities with additional mental health needs present unique challenges to health and social care professionals in detection, diagnosis and the provision of appropriate therapeutic services. This book consists of 12 chapters written by experienced clinicians who highlight the themes of policy and practice using the available evidence base to describe examples of good practice illustrated by individual cases. We believe that this book will be useful to a wide range of professionals such as child and adolescent psychiatrists, psychologists in health and educational services, nurses (children's nurses, school nurses, mental health and intellectual disability nurses), social workers, teachers, service commissioners and providers.

The nature, prevalence and causes of intellectual disability and mental health disorders are considered in Chapter 2, laying the foundations of a basic understanding of the wide needs of this group of young people. The main focus of Chapter 3 is on forensic practice, recognising the high prevalence of intellectual disabilities among young people in custody compared to the general population. The importance of assessing risk from a structured perspective for those young people within forensic services is addressed.

Children and young people with intellectual disabilities present specific conditions and behaviour problems, and these are discussed in Chapter 4. We have considered specific assessments and diagnostic issues from a comprehensive multidisciplinary approach to include psychological, functional, communication and occupational therapy perspectives, which are all covered in Chapters 5, 6, 7 and 8.

Chapter 9 provides an overview on psychological interventions, recognising the need to adapt general interventions and approaches for this group of young people. Chapter 10 reviews the limited evidence for psychopharmacological interventions and describes the basic principles involved in ensuring good clinical practice in this poorly researched area. Chapter 11 explores the development of child and adolescent mental health services for young people with intellectual disabilities and mental health needs, and looks at the national policy of providing personalised community-based servicers.

Transition from school to adult services continues to be a major problem for children and young people with intellectual disabilities and their families. Families and the young person's involvement in transition planning networks have a major impact in achieving successful outcomes, and this is considered in Chapter 12.

We very much hope you value the richness of this book in your daily practice and that we can build on the reflection of our own practice to increase the evidence base, so improving the lives and outcomes for all young people with intellectual disabilities in need of mental health care.

References

Department for Education (DfE) (2018) *Working together to safeguard children: a guide to inter-agency working to safeguard and promote the welfare of children*. London: HM Government.

Dura Villa G & Hodes M (2012) Ethnic factors in mental health service utilisation among people with intellectual disability in high-income countries: systematic review. *Journal of Intellectual Disability Research* **56** 827–842.

Eisenhower A & Blacher J (2006). Mothers of young adults with intellectual disability: multiple roles, ethnicity and well-being. *Journal of Intellectual Disability Research* **50** 905–916.

Emerson E, Robertson J & Wood J (2004) Levels of psychological distress experienced by family carers of children and adolescents with intellectual disabilities in an urban conurbation. *Journal of Applied Research in Intellectual Disabilities* **17** 77–84.

Emerson E & Hatton C (2007) Mental health of children and adolescents with intellectual disabilities in Britain. *British Journal of Psychiatry* **191** 493–9.

Hatton C, Emerson E, Kirby S, Kotwal H, Baines S, Hutchison C, Dobson C & Marks B (2010) Majority and minority ethnic family carers of adults with intellectual disabilities: perceptions of challenging behaviour and family impact. *Journal of Applied Research in Intellectual Disabilities* **23** 63–74.

Jones L, Bellis M, Wood S, Hughes K, McCoy E, Eckley L, Bates G, Mikton C, Shakespeare T & Officer A (2012) Prevalence and risk of violence against children with disabilities: a systematic review and meta-analysis of observational studies. *Lancet* **380** (9845) 899–907.

McCann E, Lee R & Brown M (2016) The experiences and support needs of people with intellectual disabilities who identify as LGBT: a review of the literature. *Research in Developmental Disabilities* **57** 39–53.

NSPCC (2016) *Deaf and Disabled Children: Learning from case reviews.* London NSPCC.

Raghavan R & Pawson N (2010) Ethnicity and diversity. In: R Raghavan, S Bernard and J McCarthy (Eds) *Mental Health Needs of Children and Young People with Intellectual disabilities*. Pavilion Publishing and Media: Hove, UK.

Vereenooghe L, Flynn S, Hastings RP *et al* (2018) Interventions for mental health problems in children and adults with severe intellectual disabilities: a systematic review. *BMJ Open* **8** (6) e021911.

Wilson NJ, Macdonald J, Hayman B, Bright AM, Frawley P & Gallego G (2016) A narrative review of the literature about people with intellectual disability who identify as lesbian, gay, bisexual, transgender, intersex or questioning. *Journal of Intellectual Disabilities* **22** 171–196.

Chapter 2: Epidemiology and aetiology

Dr Sarah H Bernard

Chapter summary

The focus of this chapter is to offer an overview of the epidemiology and aetiology of children and adolescents with intellectual disabilities. A range of epidemiological studies will be considered and aetiological factors reviewed. This chapter does not attempt to provide a comprehensive account of the molecular or clinical genetics of the aetiology of intellectual disability, or an account of the multitude of syndromes associated with intellectual disability, as this is beyond the scope of this book.

Introduction

'Intellectual disability' refers to a global impairment of intellectual and adaptive functions arising in the developmental period, along with an IQ below 70. The terminology used is dependent on a number of factors. 'Learning disability' was the term used mainly in the UK and was adopted by the Department of Health, while 'mental retardation' is more commonly used across the world in scientific literature. The term 'intellectual disability' has been used inter-changeably in place of 'mental retardation' and is now being used more widely in the UK, Europe and the US. 'Developmental disability' is the other term used, but this may include people without intellectual disability or mental retardation. The term 'intellectual disability' will be used in this book.

For a diagnosis of intellectual disability to be made, the intellectual impairment should have arisen in the developmental period, either in utero or during childhood or adolescence. Traditionally, the diagnosis of intellectual disability was made when an IQ score was below 70 on a psychometric assessment. The degree of intellectual disability is further classified into four groups based on IQ (see Table 2.1). More recently, the diagnosis has been based on the impairment of functional or adaptive skills, rather than on IQ scores alone.

Definition of intellectual disability

Psychiatric disorders are diagnosed when well-defined symptoms and signs are present for a minimum specified duration (referred to as diagnostic criteria). Disorders are diagnosed using one of the two major classification systems:

- The International Statistical Classification of Diseases and Related Health Problems 10th Revision (ICD-10) Classification of Mental and Behavioural Disorders (WHO, 1992)
- Diagnostic and Statistical Manual of Mental Disorders – Fifth Edition Text Revision (DSM-IV-TR) (APA, 2012)

The ICD-10 is the system of classification commonly used in the UK, although some centres of research use DSM-IV-TR. The ICD-10 defines 'mental retardation' (or intellectual disability) as:

'*A condition of arrested or incomplete development of the mind characterised by impairment of skills manifested during the developmental period, which contribute to the overall level of intelligence i.e. cognitive, language, motor and social abilities.*' (WHO, 1992)

Table 2.1: The four categories of intellectual disability	
Categories	IQ
Mild	50-69
Moderate	35-49
Severe	20-34
Profound	<20

Adapted from The ICD-10 Classification of Mental and Behavioural Disorders (WHO, 1992)

Although the ICD-10 diagnostic categories are defined in terms of IQ, they are based on an overall level of adaptive and functional skills. Onset in the developmental period is crucial in making a diagnosis.

Readers should be aware of changes in definitions when the ICD-11 is implemented in 2022.

Epidemiology of intellectual disability

Children and adolescents with developmental disabilities are at an increased risk of developing mental health or behavioural problems when compared to their non-disabled peers. This fact is supported by several epidemiological studies. A landmark study of children aged 10–12 on the Isle of Wight demonstrated that emotional and behavioural disorders were much more common in children with intellectual disabilities (Rutter *et al*, 1970). In addition, a study of children with severe intellectual disability aged 0–15 years in southeast London demonstrated that 47% of children were shown to have some form of psychiatric disorder (Corbett, 1979). In Sweden, a study of 13–17 year olds demonstrated increased rates of autism, language and social impairment and psychosis in those with an IQ of less than 50 (Gillberg *et al*, 1986).

More recently, Emerson and Hatton, in their study of 641 children with intellectual disabilities, demonstrated higher rates of social disadvantage and an increased risk of all psychiatric disorders (Emerson & Hatton, 2007). It is also recognised that these children are less likely to access appropriate mental health services. Even when they do, their psychiatric and developmental needs are not readily recognised, understood or addressed in an evidence-based manner.

Research findings are consistent, with a third of children and young people with intellectual disability experiencing mental health problems, compared with 11% of those who have only a physical disability or chronic illness, and eight per cent of children and young people in the general population. In a single London borough where the population is approximately 250,000 – 20% of these being children and young people (approximately 50,000) – one should expect two to three per cent (approximately 1,500) to have an intellectual disability, with approximately 250 of these having an IQ of less than 50. A third of those with multiple disabilities will have mental health problems that are diagnosable and treatable, and if left untreated will inevitably lead to a significantly impaired quality of life and underachievement. This is approximately 420 individuals. Half of those with severe learning difficulties will have mental health problems that are both diagnosable and manageable, constituting a further 125 individuals. Thus, at any time there are approximately 550 children and young people in just one London borough who have an intellectual disability requiring mental health assessment and treatment (Bernard & Turk, 2009).

According to Fryers and Russell (2003), considerable variation is reported in the prevalence rates of intellectual disability across gender and socio-economic strata (more common in males and in lower socio-economic populations), geographical regions, time periods (even within the same population) and age groups.

The prevalence of severe intellectual disability is estimated to be three to four persons per 1,000, accounting for 10–20% of people with intellectual disability. Thirty people per 1,000 of the population have mild intellectual disabilities (IQ 50–69) and three per 1,000 have moderate intellectual disabilities (IQ 35–49) (Fryers & Russell, 2003).

The aetiology of intellectual disability

The aetiology of intellectual disability will be a combination of genetic, organic and psychosocial causes. In general, prenatal and perinatal aetiological factors are primarily genetic or organic. Such factors include chromosomal and single gene defects, toxins and infections, metabolic disorders, hypoxia and trauma. After birth, the combined effects of genetic factors and psychosocial causes come into play. The latter includes profound deprivation, abuse and neglect.

The understanding of the genetic causes of intellectual disability is a fast-moving area of research. Many genes have been implicated, and understanding has been progressed with a number of large-scale genetic studies and extensive research in genomics (Mir & Kuchay, 2018). Guidance has been developed to assist in decisions about diagnostic pathways and appropriate investigations (Srour & Shevell, 2013).

Causes in prenatal, perinatal and postnatal stages

Genetic causes:

- Chromosomal
- Single gene abnormality
- Inborn errors of metabolism

Infections:

- Toxoplasmosis
- Cytomegalovirus
- Rubella
- Toxins
- Alcohol
- Drug ingestion

Birth injury:

- Infections – herpes
- Perinatal hypoxia

Early childhood:

■ Infections – meningitis, encephalitis

■ Trauma

Physical conditions commonly associated with children and adolescents with intellectual disabilities

The prevalence of both physical disorders and mental health and behavioural disorders (including challenging behaviour) is increased in persons with intellectual disabilities. The physical conditions or disorders commonly seen in persons with intellectual disabilities include sensory impairment, neurological disorders (e.g. epilepsy, cerebral palsy, metabolic disorders), dental problems, obesity, cardiovascular abnormalities e.g. structural cardiac defects, and gastrointestinal disorders including constipation and reflux oesophagitis.

Risk factors and mental health problems in children with intellectual disability

Kokentausta *et al* (2007) identified the following risk factors for psychiatric disturbance in children with intellectual disability:

■ Male gender.

■ Increasing age.

■ Low socio-economic status.

■ Reduced household income.

■ Living with one biological parent.

■ Living in an institution.

■ Poor social skills.

■ Poor daily living skills.

■ Poor communication skills.

■ Moderate intellectual disability/decreasing IQ.

■ Epilepsy.

■ Specific genetic syndrome (e.g. fragile X syndrome).

The prevalence of mental health problems in children with intellectual disability

Prevalence figures for psychiatric and behavioural disorders in children with intellectual disability have varied across studies as a number of issues have been identified (Dykens, 2000). Some factors are similar to those in studies of the general population, while others are specific to people with a intellectual disability.

Factors affecting prevalence of mental health problems in children with intellectual disability are:

- severity of intellectual disability

- presence of co-morbid disorders such as autism

- setting of the study – whether the study was population based, clinic based or based on people in residential settings

- aetiology of intellectual disability, as certain disorders (e.g. genetic) are associated with specific behavioural phenotypes

- instruments used to measure psychopathology – use of instruments not standardised for use in this population affects results

- diagnostic criteria used – the existing international classificatory systems depend on language-based criteria for diagnosis and have limited utility with severely disabled individuals who may not be able to use language

- ethical considerations – some studies may not include people who are unable to consent and this distorts the true prevalence rates

- information gathering usually depends on relying on carers or family – though this may improve the quality of information available, it may also introduce recall bias

- difficulty distinguishing behaviours related to mental health problems from 'challenging behaviour' – this is a common problem as it may be difficult to distinguish 'behavioural problems' from behaviours due to mental illness.

These studies, and others, reflect the need to be mindful of the biopsychosocial model when considering the cause of an intellectual disability. In addition, how these multifactorial causative factors impact on psychiatric or behavioural disturbance should be part of diagnostic formulations and care planning.

Case studies of prevalence

The following key studies examined the prevalence of mental health problems in children with intellectual disability.

Dekker and Koot (2003) studied a random sample of 474 children with intellectual disability from Dutch schools for the intellectually disabled. Of the 474 children included in the study, 25.1% met DSM-IV criteria for disruptive behaviour, 21.9% for anxiety disorder and 4.4% for mood disorder. More than half (56%) of the children with a DSM-IV diagnosis had significant impairment in at least one area of everyday functioning, with 37% of the children having a comorbid disorder.

Emerson and Hatton (2007) studied the prevalence of ICD-10 psychiatric disorders in 18,415 British children, with and without intellectual disabilities. Measures used included the Development and Well-being Assessment (DAWBA) and the General Health Questionnaire. The authors state that, 'children with intellectual disabilities accounted for 14% of all British children with a diagnosable psychiatric disorder', with 36% of British children and adolescents with intellectual disability having a diagnosable psychiatric disorder.

When considering specific psychiatric disorders, the rate of hyperkinetic disorder in the school-age population is found to be one to two per cent, following the narrow criteria of ICD-10 with the rate for ADHD as defined in DSM-IV ranging from 3–12%, depending on diagnostic criteria. Population studies confirm a sex difference with two to three boys affected for every girl. The aetiology includes genetic causes with twin studies suggesting a heritability of 80%. Environmental factors that are implicated include smoking, drinking and maternal stress during pregnancy. The majority of those with ADHD have persisting symptoms into adult life. In children aged five to 15 years, the prevalence rate of conduct disorder is 5–15%, compared to a rate in young people with intellectual disabilities of 25% (Emerson, 2003).

In an Australian study of children with intellectual disabilities, a prevalence rate of nine per cent was reported for persistent symptoms of depression, and a rate of eight per cent for anxiety (Tonge, 2007). The prevalence of depressive symptoms was less prevalent in those with severe or profound intellectual disability, with a rate of three per cent. The prevalence of depression did not change over the 14 years considered by the study for both genders and this was also the case for anxiety disorders in the boys, but for the girls the prevalence of anxiety disorders increased to 20%.

The prevalence of psychoses in adults with intellectual disability is three per cent, which is three times greater than in the general population.

Syndromal causes of intellectual disability and behavioural phenotypes

There are a multitude of syndromes that have an associated intellectual disability. Many have a well-defined physical phenotype, for example Down's syndrome. Some also have a behavioural phenotype such as Prader Willi syndrome or fragile-X syndrome (Beadsmore *et al*, 1998; Bergman *et al*, 1988; Deb, 1997). A knowledge of the behaviours and the likelihood of developing a psychiatric disorder associated with specific syndromes is important in order to provide early intervention and reduce avoidable risk factors (Waite *et al*, 2014).

Conclusion

An understanding of the epidemiology and aetiology of developmental disability in childhood is essential when considering the mental health or behavioural difficulties of children and young people with intellectual disabilities. This understanding informs service provision and enables preventative aspects of care to be considered.

References

American Psychiatric Association (2000) *Diagnostic and Statistical Manual of Mental Disorders* (4th edition) Washington, DC: American Psychiatric Association.

Beadsmore K, Dormamn T, Cooper SA & Webb T (1998) Affective psychosis and Prader-Willi syndrome. *Journal of Intellectual Disability Research* (6) 463–471.

Bergman JD, Leckman JF & Ort SJ (1988) Fragile X syndrome: genetic predisposition to psychopathology. *Journal of Autism and Developmental Disorders* 343–354.

Bernard SH & Turk J (2009) *Developing Mental Health Services for Children and Adolescents with Intellectual disabilities: A toolkit for clinicians*. London: Royal College of Psychiatrists.

Corbett JA (1979) Population studies in mental retardation. In: P Graham (Ed) *Epidemiology of Child Psychiatry*. London: Academic Press.

Deb S (1997) Behavioural phenotypes. In: S Reed (Ed) *Psychiatry in Intellectual disabilities*. London: WB Saunders Company Ltd.

Dekker MC & Koot HM (2003) DSM-IV disorders in children with borderline to moderate intellectual disability. *Journal of the American Academy of Child and Adolescent Psychiatry* (8) 923–931.

Dykens EM (2000) Annotation: psychopathology in children with intellectual disability. *Journal of Child Psychology and Psychiatry* (4) 407–417.

Dykens EM, Leckman JF & Cassidy SB (1996) Obsessions and compulsions in Prader-Willi syndrome. *Journal of Child Psychology and Psychiatry* 995–1002.

Emerson (2003) Prevalence of psychiatric disorders in children and adolescents with and without intellectual disability. *Journal of Intellectual Disability Research* 51–58.

Emerson E & Hatton C (2007) Contribution of socioeconomic position to health inequalities of British children and adolescents with intellectual disabilities. *American Journal of Mental Retardation* 140–150.

Fryers T & Russell O (2003) *Applied Epidemiology: Seminars in the psychiatry of intellectual disabilities* (2nd edition). London: Royal College of Psychiatrists.

Gillberg C, Persson U, Grufman M & Temner U (1986) Psychiatric disorders in mildly and severely mentally retarded urban children and adolescents. Epidemiological aspects. *British Journal of Psychiatry* 69–88.

Kokentausta T, Livanainen M & Almqvist F (2007) Risk factors for psychiatric disturbance in children with intellectual disability. *Journal of Intellectual Disability Research* (1) 43–53.

Martin JP & Bell J (1943) A pedigree of mental defect showing sex linkage. *Journal of Neurology and Psychiatry* 154–160.

Mefford HC, Batshaw ML, Hoffman EP (2012) Genomics, intellectual disability, and autism. *New England Journal of Medicine* **366** (8) 733–743.

Rutter M, Graham P & Yule W (1970) A neuropsychiatric study in childhood. Clinics in developmental medicine. *Clinics in Developmental Medicine.*

Tonge B (2007) The psychopathology of children with intellectual disabilities. In: N Bouras & G Holt (Eds) *Psychiatric and Behavioural Disorders in Intellectual and Developmental Disabilities* (2nd edition). Cambridge: Cambridge University Press.

Waite M, Heald L, Wilde K, Woodcock A, Adams D & Chris O (2014) The importance of understanding the behavioural phenotypes of genetic syndromes associated with intellectual disability. *Paediatrics and Child Health* **24** (10) 468–472

World Health Organization (1992) *The ICD–10 Classification of Mental and Behavioural Disorders: Clinical descriptions and diagnostic guidelines.* Geneva: WHO.

Zigman W, Schupf N, Haveman M & Silverman W (1995) *Epidemiology of Alzheimer's Disease in Mental Retardation: Results and recommendations from an international conference.* Washington DC: AAMR.

Chapter 3: Forensic issues

Kate Johnston & Troy Tranah

Chapter summary

This chapter describes the forensic issues affecting young people with intellectual disabilities, focusing on prevalence and types of offences, including patterns of offences. It outlines approaches to risk assessment and formulation, and it provides an overview of interventions, including interventions for harmful sexual behaviours and aggression. The chapter considers assessment of the young person when required for the purpose of court and legal proceedings, including the ability for the young person to stand trial. Finally, the chapter uses a case vignette to illustrate the steps from assessment to formulation to intervention.

Introduction

In the UK, young people with intellectual disability are overrepresented at all stages of the criminal justice system. In particular, the prevalence of intellectual disability among children in custody has been found to be 23-32%, compared to rates of 2-4% in the general population (Hughes *et al*, 2012). It is also important to note the high prevalence and comorbidity of related disorders such as ADHD, specific learning difficulties (e.g. dyslexia), speech and language disorders and traumatic brain injury. Additionally, there are a group of adolescents with borderline cognitive functioning (IQ between 70 and 80) who do not meet the diagnostic criteria for a intellectual disability, but who may present with similar forensic issues. In the UK, one study that assessed 301 young offenders in custody using a screening measure, found that 41% had borderline IQ (Chitsabesan *et al*, 2007). It is therefore important that practitioners have a good understanding of forensic issues affecting young people with intellectual disabilities.

Offending by young people with intellectual disabilities

Young people with 'mild' intellectual disabilities are more likely to come into contact with the criminal justice system than those with moderate to profound disability.

It has been suggested that this often means that such young people will have had unidentified, and therefore unmet, needs at school/in the community.

In adults, some studies have found that the prevalence of specific types of offending (arson and sexual offences) are higher in intellectual disability samples, although these are by no means consistent findings. In children and adolescents, some studies also support a slightly differing pattern of offending among those with intellectual disabilities relative to their peers. For instance, young offenders aged 12-18 diagnosed with a global intellectual disability in the US were more likely to have committed offences against the person (e.g. assault, threats of harm) than young offenders without ID. Within services for adolescents with harmful sexual behaviour (HSB), it is thought that between 24% and 38% have intellectual disabilities (Vizard *et al*, 2007; Hackett *et al*, 2013), which is a significant overrepresentation relative to the prevalence of ID in the general population. Young people with ID who display HSB have been found to be less 'gender specific' in their offending than those without ID (Balogh *et al*, 2001). Their offending is also generally found to be more impulsive than their non-ID peers and to include higher rates of 'nuisance' offences (e.g. exposure) (Almond & Giles, 2008). However, the same study (Almond & Giles, 2008), which compared 51 young people with ID and 51 without ID who had displayed HSB, found that both groups were broadly similar in terms of victim and perpetrator characteristics. Reviews have suggested that between a third to a half of young people who sexually offend have a intellectual disability; significantly higher than rates of ID in adult sex offender samples.

Relatedly, rates of inappropriate and harmful sexual behaviour have been found to be very high in a survey of UK special schools, with 88% reporting this having occurred in their setting (Fyson, 2007). Most common issues were public masturbation (58%) and inappropriate touching (85%). The management of inappropriate/harmful sexual behaviours is often a challenging area for those working with this client group and a common difficulty is knowing when behaviours warrant intervention (Fyson, 2007).

Several studies have explored the reason for these differing patterns of offending. There is a risk of increased rates of anger and aggression in individuals with intellectual disabilities (Novaco & Taylor, 2004), which in turn increases the risk of violent offending. Offenders with ID will often have deficits in information processing and social/communication skills which, in combination with poor self-regulation and higher levels of impulsivity, may explain high rates of aggression and offences against the person. Adolescents with ID are also at higher risk than their non-ID peers for delinquency, meaning that exposure to systemic/environmental risk factors for offending are higher.

Adolescents with intellectual disabilities are more likely to be vulnerable to criminal and sexual exploitation, meaning that they may come into contact with the criminal justice system for offences such as drug or weapon possession having been manipulated into various offences to gain social acceptance, status, protection or tangible rewards such as money or drugs. Recent UK government guidance for practitioners specifically notes that learning and/or physical disabilities is a key risk factor for such exploitation via 'county lines' (HM Government, 2018). The same is true for child sexual exploitation. The risk or severity of child sexual exploitation in young people with a intellectual disability can be assessed using the SERAF assessment tool (Coles & Clutton, 2008). Criminal and/or sexual exploitation should be considered within existing safeguarding frameworks.

In relation to sexual offending, young people with ID are known to experience high rates of abuse (including sexual abuse) relative to their non-disabled peers. Disability is also associated with longer durations of such abuse. While not all young people who are victims of abuse will go on to offend, this is a significant risk factor for all sexual offenders (Vizard, 2007). There are also important societal factors including prejudice and misunderstanding in relation to normative sexual development and sexuality for individuals with intellectual disability. This is often combined with reduced access to appropriate sex and relationship education in schools, meaning that young people may not be equipped to understand and manage puberty and sexual development. Evidence-based risk factors for sexual offending, such as poor social skills, are also more common in those with ID relative to the general population. It is important to note that research data is largely drawn from specific clinical services for young people who have committed sexual abuse and so is likely to be biased. This data does not support the idea that young people with intellectual disabilities have a specific predisposition to sexual offending.

Forensic and risk assessment in young people with intellectual disabilities

Assessment of young people with intellectual disabilities and forensic issues should ideally be comprehensive and include a mental health assessment, risk assessment and full cognitive assessment where possible. This should lead to the development of a psychological formulation of presenting issues. A detailed family and developmental history may also be helpful, and clinicians should remember to think and ask about the possibility that the young person may be the victim of abuse (Vizard, 2013) or exploitation. Of note, there has been very little research into the area of risk assessment for children and adolescents with intellectual disabilities, which can cause significant difficulties for practitioners working in this area. Pragmatic use of tools designed for adults with intellectual disabilities, or adolescents without disabilities is common. Despite this not being an optimal approach, there is also a counter argument that young people with intellectual disabilities may share a number of risk factors for offending with their non-disabled peers and so using a validated, evidence-based risk assessment may be beneficial.

Boer *et al* (2010) suggest that in adults there is no evidence of reliability of structured professional judgement risk assessment tools for individuals with IQ scores below 55, and the same conclusion is likely to apply to child and adolescent samples.

Violence/aggression

There are no standardised risk assessments for young people with intellectual disabilities who have displayed violent/aggressive behaviour. In young people with moderate or severe intellectual disabilities, such behaviours may be best conceptualised as behaviours that challenge and evaluated using a functional assessment approach. For those with mild or borderline intellectual disabilities, it may be appropriate to use a structured professional judgement tool such as the SAVRY, noting the presence of a intellectual disability as an additional item. Adamson *et al* (2011) note that there are specific factors in general adolescent risk assessment tools which may have different predictive utility in young people with intellectual disabilities. These include items such as 'poor school achievement' in the SAVRY. Clinicians should therefore be cautious in scoring and interpreting such items.

In assessing risk of future violence in young people with intellectual disabilities, it is important to gather information from a range of sources, including family/carers, the young person, their school and placement (if relevant) in order to identify any specific triggers/patterns as well as ensuring a holistic view of the young person.

Sexualised behaviour

There are no validated measures for the assessment of inappropriate or harmful sexual behaviour for children and adolescents with intellectual disabilities. The AIM (Assessment, Intervention, Moving on) has been adapted for use with young people with intellectual disabilities by modifying the scoring system, however a study by Griffin and Vettor (2012) established that both the adapted AIM and AIM 2 showed good accuracy in identifying adolescents who sexually reoffend. The authors concluded therefore that adolescents who display harmful sexual behaviour do not require specific risk assessment tools.

In order to assess inappropriate or harmful sexualised behaviour in this population, it may be useful to first consider what is developmentally/age appropriate, particularly given societal views about sex and the sexuality of individuals with intellectual disabilities. Use of the 'Traffic Lights Tool' from Brook[1] can be useful

---

1   https://legacy.brook.org.uk/brook_tools/traffic/Brook_Traffic_Light_Tool.pdf

in establishing the appropriateness or otherwise of sexualised behaviours. In assessing young people with a intellectual disability who have displayed harmful sexual behaviours, it will generally be necessary to offer an extended assessment period (over several sessions) in order to gain a full understanding of issues such as consent, sexual knowledge and any past history of sexual abuse.

Interventions

There is a paucity of evidence-based psychological interventions for young people with intellectual disabilities and forensic presentations. Most research has been conducted into interventions for harmful sexual behaviours. These interventions are strengths-focused approaches, aiming to both reduce risk and increase existing strengths in order to reduce the likelihood of recidivism. Cognitive-behavioural interventions have most often been used to address anger/aggression in children and adolescents with intellectual disabilities, and there is a small literature on adapted 'third wave' CBT interventions. Any intervention with a young person with a intellectual disability who has 'forensic' difficulties should include multi-agency work. As outlined above, contact with the criminal justice system may provide the first opportunity for a young person to receive a comprehensive assessment of their needs and a suitably adapted treatment programme.

Harmful sexual behaviour

The Good Way (Ayland & West, 2007) and Good Lives (Ward & Gannon, 2006) models are both strengths-focused interventions designed for use with adolescents with intellectual disabilities who have displayed harmful sexual behaviour. Both programmes adopt a narrative approach whereby young people identify their old life/bad way and work towards goals for their new life/good way. Within these frameworks, harmful sexual behaviour displayed by young people with intellectual disabilities is considered to serve a function/meet a need, albeit in a maladaptive way. Risk factors are identified and coping strategies or skills are taught. Both approaches also include trauma-focused work and relapse prevention, and are adapted to include the use of visual materials, developmentally appropriate language, and to draw on the resource of the wider network/system around the young person. To date there is a small research literature suggesting that both models can engage young people in therapeutic work and reduce further incidents of harmful sexual behaviour. There is, however, a lack of rigorous research evidence.

In the UK, the Keep Safe intervention (Malovic et al, 2018) is a manualised group-based CBT intervention for adolescents with intellectual disabilities and harmful sexual behaviour. Keep Safe includes components from both the Good Way and Good Lives models as well as other group CBT interventions (e.g. Carpentier et al, 2006). The Keep Safe intervention has been evaluated with a small number of adolescents with moderate intellectual disabilities (IQ 43–56) with preliminary evidence of acceptability and feasibility with this group.

Anger/aggression

There is a small literature on adapted CBT for anger/aggression from adult forensic intellectual disability populations suggesting that this can be an effective approach, with similar effect sizes to the general population (Nicoll et al, 2013). Adapted CBT has also been found to be useful for adolescents with intellectual disabilities and a range of emotional/mental health difficulties that are non-forensic in nature.

In adults with mild-moderate intellectual disabilities, there is preliminary evidence to suggest that adapted dialectical behaviour therapy (DBT) skills groups may be beneficial in reducing aggressive or violent behaviour in forensic settings. Of note, one study found that the adapted DBT skills intervention reduced risk but also increased strengths in this population (Sakdalan et al, 2010). Similarly, mindfulness has been shown to be effective in reducing physical and verbal aggression in adults with mild intellectual disabilities in a wait-list control trial (Singh et al, 2013). There are no such published studies for adolescents with intellectual disabilities, but using an adapted DBT skills approach may be beneficial for young people whose behaviour appears to be driven by difficulties in emotion regulation.

Environmental interventions may be more appropriate in some cases (e.g. a specialist therapeutic placement) and young people with more severe intellectual disabilities may best be supported via positive behaviour support interventions designed to enhance strengths and improve quality of life for the individual and those around them.

Criminal justice system

Children and adolescents with intellectual disabilities may come into contact with the criminal justice system (CJS) as victims of crime (especially abuse) or as defendants. Research has shown that people with ID are more suggestible during police interviews than the general population (Clare & Gudjonsson, 1995), as well as having more global difficulties in understanding complex language, and so it is important to ensure that appropriate measures are put in place to support people with ID at various points in the criminal justice process. If a young person with ID is arrested and/or questioned by the police, an appropriate adult (AA) should be present. The role of the AA is to be an advisor to the person being interviewed, to observe the interview and ensure that it is being conducted fairly and properly, and to facilitate communication between the person with ID and the interviewer.

If a young person with ID is to be charged with a criminal offence, there may be the need for an assessment of fitness to plead. In the UK, fitness to plead is based on case law (*R vs Pritchard*, 1836). In order to be fit to plead, a defendant must understand the charge(s) against them, decide whether to plead guilty or not guilty, understand and be able to challenge jurors, instruct solicitors, follow the proceedings in court and give evidence in his/her own defence. Without one or more of these abilities, a conventional trial should not proceed (*R v Podola*, 1960). A further consideration for young defendants with intellectual disability is whether or not they have the ability to 'effectively participate' in a trial, something which is enshrined in Article 6 of the European Convention on Human Rights (right to a fair trial).

In the US, standardised assessment measures exist in relation to this ability (e.g. MCAT-CA), based on the Grisso criteria. These are:

1. Understanding of charges and potential consequences:
   - Ability to understand and appreciate the charges and their seriousness.
   - Ability to understand possible consequences of potential pleas.
   - Ability to appraise realistically the likely outcome.

2. Understanding the trial process:
   - Ability to understand, without significant distortion, the roles of participants in the trial process (e.g. judge, defence lawyer, prosecutor, witness, jury).
   - Ability to understand the process and potential consequences of pleading.
   - Ability to grasp the general sequence of pre-trial/trial events.

3. Capacity to participate with a lawyer in a defence:
   - Ability to trust adequately or work collaboratively with a lawyer.
   - Ability to disclose to the lawyer reasonably coherent description of the facts relating to the charges, as perceived by the defendant.
   - Ability to reason about available options by weighing consequences, without significant distortion.
   - Ability to challenge realistically prosecution witnesses and monitor trial events.

4. Potential for Court Room Participation:
   - Ability to testify coherently, if testimony is needed.
   - Ability to control own behaviour during trial proceedings.
   - Ability to manage the stress of trial.

In assessing a young person with ID who is to stand trial, understanding the above criteria is essential. Talbot (2009) suggests that there is always a need for a full cognitive assessment before a young person with a diagnosed or suspected intellectual disability stands trial. This should include not only IQ but also memory, attention and language, as these may have a significant impact on the ability to participate in a trial.

Although vulnerable witnesses or victims of crime can be supported by various 'special measures', such as giving evidence via video-link, pre-recorded cross examination and/or evidence in chief, and having the support of a registered intermediary, these supports are not routinely in place for vulnerable young defendants. To date, there is also no published research evidence to establish whether such special measures improve the quality of evidence provided or increase the ability to participate in trial.

Conclusions

Young people with intellectual disabilities are over-represented at all stages of the criminal justice system and are also highly vulnerable to being victims of crime, including child criminal/sexual exploitation. Despite this, there is a dearth of research into appropriate risk assessments and interventions with this population. The evidence available suggests that cautious use of existing risk assessment tools is appropriate alongside comprehensive psychiatric/psychological assessment by an experienced professional. Preliminary data suggests that adapted cognitive behavioural and narrative approaches may be effective at engaging young people in psychological treatment designed to build strengths and reduce risk, particularly in terms of those who have engaged in harmful sexual behaviour. There is a very significant lack of treatment studies for young people who have committed violent offences. Clinicians working with young people with intellectual disabilities and 'forensic' behaviours should always consider conducting a comprehensive assessment, using multiple informants where possible, to build a holistic picture of the young person and the drivers behind their behaviour. Adopting a formulation-driven approach to intervention, drawing on relevant adult ID literature and/or non-ID offender literature is likely to be the most pragmatic approach to reducing the risk of reoffending.

Case vignette

George (a pseudonym) was a White British 16-year-old boy with a mild intellectual disability and ADHD who came into contact with services after being arrested for an arson offence. It subsequently came to light that he had also set another fire in the recent past which had not come to police attention. He had previously attended a mainstream school where his intellectual disability and ADHD was undiagnosed and unsupported. There was an extensive history of bullying and George had no friends, limited social contact and described himself as the 'odd one out'. He had not passed any GCSE exams and had taken on a variety of low paid jobs, which he left frequently. George had begun attending his local church approximately one year before the arson offence and reported that he had a number of friends from church, all of whom were elderly women. He also attended a church group for older people but was asked to stop attending the day before the arson offence due to him disrupting the group by frequently telling exaggerated stories about acts of aggression. There were also multiple reports from the churchwarden that George repeatedly 'discovered' minor acts of vandalism in and around the church which were thought to be caused by him.

Assessment

At assessment, George reported a long history of anxiety with poor coping mechanisms. A cognitive assessment revealed a FSIQ of 62 with corresponding difficulties in adaptive behaviour. There were also notable speech and language difficulties. George was diagnosed with an intellectual disability and ADHD.

A functional assessment of George's arson offence was undertaken over three 1:1 sessions. Information was also taken from relevant background papers and talking with George's parents. George was observed by witnesses at the scene of the fire to be excited and 'hyped up', talking a lot, excitable, flitting from topic to topic, and seeming invigorated by it. Police records stated: '[I had] formed the view that he liked being the centre of attention as he had information'. George told one witness he was from Neighbourhood Watch and went on to talk about himself a lot including 'fantastical stories' e.g. that he was a famous artist, could fly a helicopter etc. He also claimed that he had received an anonymous telephone call about the fire despite phone records disputing this.

A relative had died in a house fire when George was young.

Formulation

A collaborative formulation was developed in which fire-setting behaviour was understood as being motivated by George's feelings of anger and frustration and his inability to express or cope with these emotions in a more adaptive way.

At the time of the fire George appears to have been socially isolated, bored and poorly supervised. George described feeling the 'odd one out' since early childhood. He has a lifelong difficulty in making friends of his own age and getting along with work colleagues. He commented that his speech and language difficulties made it difficult for him to fit in at school and he reports experiencing bullying from peers. George's parents report that he did not have any friends or social contact at the time of the fire other than attending church on a weekly basis.

George was not engaged in any meaningful activity at the time of the fire and appears to lack those skills which would make him employable. George does not appear to have been engaged in activities which gave him a sense of mastery and pleasure and his overall description of his life before the fire was that he was 'bored'. He has a history of poor tolerance of frustration and some difficulty with controlling his anger. Historically, George also appears to have poor coping mechanisms for dealing with anxiety.

George's fire-setting behaviour does not appear to have been primarily motivated by a sensory or sexual interest in fire, although he reported finding the colour/flames of the second fire exciting. Fire setting appears to have been a consequence of George's anger and frustration triggered by an argument with a senior member of his church. The threat of losing contact with the church was significant as this was his only source of social contact and a place where he had created a role which gave him a sense of mastery and pleasure. In response to this anger and anxiety, George lit the first fire. His description of events suggests he may have felt a sense of power and excitement. Once the fire had been extinguished, he adopted a 'helper' role in boarding up the building, again giving him a sense of responsibility and importance. It is hypothesised that George's fire setting was reinforced by these experiences. He may have been seeking similar reinforcement when he started the second fire.

The arson appears to have been a functional behaviour, perhaps also motivated by George's desire to gain social attention. Being the centre of attention may also have acted to raise George's self-esteem, albeit temporarily, as he appears to have felt as though he was fulfilling a role in events surrounding the fire. George reports that following being asked to stop attending the church group, he felt very negative about himself and his abilities as well as feeling angry.

An additional function of the fire setting was to provide George with a means of excitement. He was described by witnesses as being 'hyped up' and excited at the scene of the fire and this may well have been in contrast to his everyday routine, which appears to have lacked stimulating or pleasurable events.

George has a history of similar but less serious behaviours which could be considered within the same functional class as his fire-setting behaviour. These include what he referred to as 'story telling' and reports from the churchwarden that he often 'discovered' minor damage in the church. On one occasion he was clearly seen but said it must have been 'another person in identical clothes'. The description of George's behaviour at the scene of the fire may be indicative of his wanting to gain social attention from others in a similar way to that described by members of his church. He also appeared subjectively to find the fire and associated activities exciting.

Intervention

Following his conviction, George was offered individual offence-focused CBT sessions. Initially he denied any involvement in setting fires but subsequently was able to give a good account of events. Offence-focused work aimed to help George develop a coherent narrative of events, including his own role in these, and to develop appropriate ways of coping with similar situations in the future.

As part of assessment and risk planning, a SAVRY was completed with an additional item added to reflect George's neurodevelopmental profile. This was used to develop a risk management plan (including reduced access to matches/lighters, supervised community use etc). George's strengths were also identified (sociability, close family, wanting to engage in intervention).

Work on emotion recognition and regulation was completed initially in order to help George to engage in cognitive-behavioural therapy. A separate focus for individual sessions was George's tendency to report multiple physical health complaints and exaggerated stories of violence/aggression, which he referred to as 'story telling'. George's 'story telling' relating to violence or aggression is in contrast to his observed behaviour. George was able to talk about these behaviours insightfully, describing his stories of fighting and violence as attempts to impress people and make friends. He commented that his storytelling actually, 'makes people stay away from you, which is not what I want'. Helping George to reflect upon these behaviours and simultaneously giving non-contingent attention has been of benefit and these behaviours reduced significantly.

George initially viewed his fire setting as 'accidental' or due to factors such as ADHD, but he was able to take responsibility for his actions during therapy. While he acknowledged the importance of anger and boredom in his offence, he did not consider social attention as an important motivating factor despite the accounts of witnesses describing him as being 'hyped up' and creating a role for himself at the scene of the fire by telling people that he was in the neighbourhood watch. Interestingly, George identified social attention as being the reason for his 'storytelling' and spoke about his desire to 'fit in' by portraying himself as being violent.

George made good progress in therapy and was able to think about ways of reducing the risk of future offending during the latter stages of treatment, including the development and practice of a daily relaxation routine to help manage anger/arousal. He was also encouraged to monitor his thoughts and feelings and to discuss any significant changes with a member of support staff.

As well as individual therapeutic work, a package of care was offered to George and his family which aimed to increase strengths and meaningful social activity.

He enrolled in a supported horticulture training programme and through this gained regular, structured activity with some social contact. Objectively, this served to increase his self-esteem and self-worth. George's parents were also offered additional support via a social work practitioner who helped them to increase their supervision of George, both in the home and in the community, to understand his intellectual disability diagnosis and to provide advice and support in engaging with community resources.

References

Adamson L, McLean A & Sher MA (2011) Risk assessment in Adolescents with Developmental Disabilities. In: E. Gralton (Ed) *Forensic Focus 32: Forensic issues in adolescents with developmental disabilities*. London: Jessica Kinglsey.

Almond L & Giles S (2008) Young people with harmful sexual behaviour: Do those with Intellectual disabilities form a distinct subgroup? *Journal of Sexual Aggression* **14** 227–239.

Ayland L & West B (2007) The Good Way model: A strengths-based approach for working with young people, especially those with intellectual disabilities, who have sexually abusive behaviour. *Journal of Sexual Aggression* **12** 189–201.

Balogh R, Bretherton K, Whibley S, Berney T, Graham S, Richold P, Worsley C & Firth H (2001) Sexual abuse in children and adolescents with intellectual disability. *Journal of Intellectual Disability Research* **45** 194–201.

Boer DP, Frize MCJ, Pappas R, Morrissey C & Lindsay WR (2010) Suggested adaptations to the HCR–20 for offenders with intellectual disabilities. In: LA Craig, WR Lindsay & KD Browne (Eds.) *Assessment and treatment of sexual offenders with intellectual disabilities: A handbook* (pp. 177–192). Chichester, England: Wiley Blackwell.

Carpentier MY, Silovsky JF & Chaffin M (2006) Randomized trial of treatment for children with sexual behaviour problems: Ten year follow up. *Journal of Consulting and Clinical Psychology* **74** 482–488.

Chitsabesan P, Bailey S, Williams R, Kroll L, Kenning C & Talbot L (2007) Intellectual disabilities and educational needs of juvenile offenders. *Journal of Children's Services*, **2** 4–17.

Clare IC & Gudjonsson GH (1995) The vulnerability of suspects with intellectual disabilities during police interviews: A review and experimental study of decision-making. *Mental Handicap Research* **8** 110–128.

Coles J & Clutton S (2008) SERAF Sexual Exploitation Risk Assessment Framework Resource Pack, Cardiff: Barnardo's Cymru.

Fyson R (2007) Young people with intellectual disabilities who sexually harm others: the role of criminal justice within a multi-agency response. *British Journal of Intellectual disabilities* **35** 181–186.

Griffin HL & Vettor S (2012) Predicting sexual re-offending in a UK sample of adolescents with intellectual disabilities. *Journal of Sexual Aggression* **18** 64–80.

Hackett S, Phillips J, Masson H & Balfe M (2013) Individual, family and abuse characteristics of 700 British child and adolescent sexual abusers. *Child Abuse Review*, **22** 232–245.

Hughes N, Williams H, Chitsabesan P, Davies R & Mounce L (2012) *Nobody Made the Connection: The prevalence of neurodisability in young people who offend*. London: Office for the Children's Commissioner.

HM Government (2018) *Criminal Exploitation of Children and Vulnerable Adults: County Lines guidance*. London: Home Office.

Malovic A, Rossiter R, Murphy GH (2018) Keep Safe: the development of a manualised group CBT intervention for adolescents with ID who display harmful sexual behaviours. *Journal of Intellectual Disabilities and Offending Behaviour* **9** 49–58.

Nicoll M, Beail N & Saxon D (2013) Cognitive behavioural treatment for anger in adults with intellectual disabilities: A systematic review and meta-analysis. *Journal of Applied Research in Intellectual Disability* **26** 47–62.

Novaco RW & Taylor JL (2004) Assessment of anger and aggression in male offenders with developmental disabilities. *Psychological Assessment* **16** 42–50.

Sakdalan JA, Shaw J & Collier V (2010) Staying in the here-and-now: A pilot study on the use of dialectical behaviour therapy group skills training for forensic clients with intellectual disability. *Journal of Intellectual Disability Research* **54** 568–572.

Singh NN, Lancioni G, Karazsia BT, Winton ASW, Myers RE, Singh ANA, Singh ADA & Singh J (2013). Mindfulness-based treatment of aggression in individuals with mild intellectual disabilities: a waiting list control study. *Mindfulness* **4** 158–167.

Talbot J (2009) No one knows: offenders with intellectual disabilities and learning difficulties. *International Journal of Prisoner Health* **5** 141–152.

Vizard E (2013) Practitioner Review: The victims and juvenile perpetrators of child sexual abuse – assessment and intervention. *Journal of Child Psychology and Psychiatry* **54** 503–515.

Vizard E, Hickey N, French L & McCrory E (2007) Children and adolescents who present with sexually abusive behaviour: A UK descriptive study. *Journal of Forensic Psychiatry and Psychology* **18** 59–73.

Ward T & Gannon TA (2006) Rehabilitation, etiology, and self-regulation: The comprehensive good lives model of treatment for sexual offenders. *Aggression and Violent Behavior* **11** 77–94.

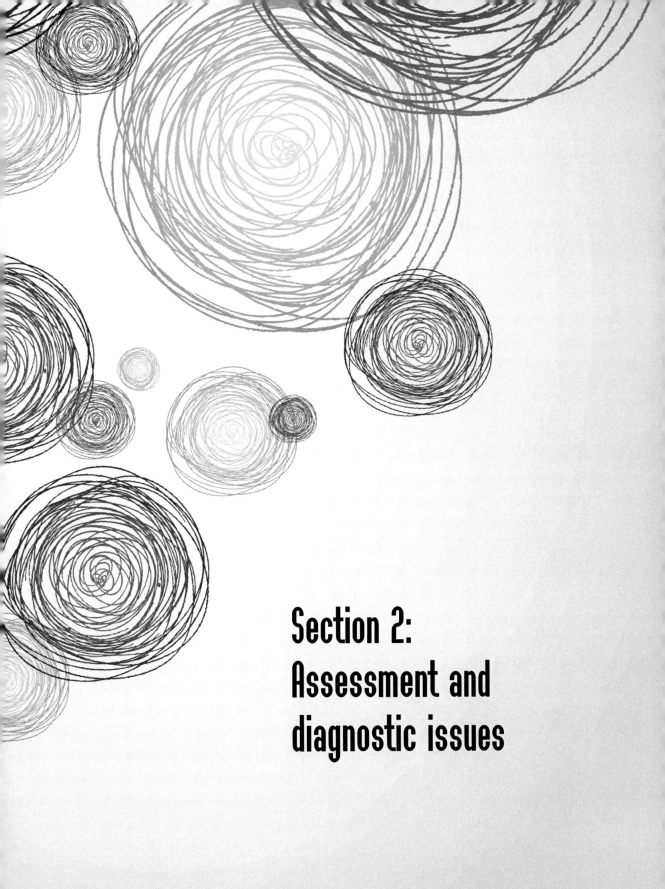

Section 2: Assessment and diagnostic issues

Chapter 4: Specific conditions

Heather Hanna

Chapter summary

This chapter describes the presentation of the most common mental health and neurodevelopmental conditions in children and adolescents with intellectual disabilities. It also considers how 'behaviours of concern', such as aggression, should be considered in the context of underlying difficulties.

Introduction

Children and adolescents with intellectual disabilities experience higher rates of mental health conditions or emotional and behavioural difficulties than their typically developing peers. This includes specific psychiatric conditions, such as mood and psychotic disorders. As the young person's degree of intellectual impairment increases, detecting and differentiating between these disorders becomes more difficult, not least because multiple co-morbidities may exist. Neurodevelopmental disorders such as autism spectrum disorder and attention deficit hyperactivity disorder (ADHD) are more common in this group of young people, further increasing the likelihood that the young person will develop emotional or behavioural difficulties or co-morbid mental health conditions (Corbett, 1977; Einfeld & Tonge, 1996).

When assessing young people with more severe intellectual disabilities and co-existing autism or ADHD, we often need to interpret a limited number of key symptoms and signs, such as irritability, withdrawal or an apparent loss of skills. The modified diagnostic classification criteria published by the Royal College of Psychiatrists, the *Diagnostic Criteria for Psychiatric Disorders for Use with Adults with Intellectual Disabilities / Mental Retardation*, is written with adults in mind but can also be helpful for the under-18 population. It recognises that, 'in clinical practice, "partial syndromes" sometimes present and clinical judgement in such circumstances is important' (Royal College of Psychiatrists, 2001). Children and young people with intellectual disabilities may present with an array of neurodevelopmental difficulties and neuropsychiatric symptoms, and recognising core groups of symptoms as part of a comprehensive formulation can be a helpful approach. The timely recognition and management of psychiatric conditions can improve a young person's developmental trajectory and quality of life.

This chapter considers specific disorders including psychotic and mood disorders, anxiety or obsessive-compulsive disorders and those specifically associated with stress. It will outline the need to specifically consider how these conditions present in the context of co-existing autism or attention deficit disorders. The psychiatric aspects of tic disorders will also be described. Sleep disorders will be considered as they are more common in children and young people with intellectual disabilities and may worsen psychiatric symptomatology.

Psychotic disorders

Psychotic disorders can be particularly difficult to detect and diagnose in young people with intellectual disabilities. Some studies suggest that the presence of psychosis in the population with intellectual disability is at least three times higher than in the general population (Aman *et al*, 2016). Often, the condition and associated impairment becomes apparent over a period of several months, with a clear change in behaviour and functional decline becoming prominent, although the sudden onset of florid hallucinations can also be seen, particularly in young people with milder intellectual disabilities. The onset of psychosis is typically in later adolescence and is very rare before the onset of puberty.

The phenomenon of self-talk is common in young people with intellectual disabilities, particularly those with autism or Down syndrome. This should not be considered pathological or an indicator of psychosis. The self-talk may include various accents or intonations, a 'two-way' conversational component and be highly animated. It can include elements of echolalia or sometimes is an opportunity for young people to 'repair' social encounters where they felt frustrated. The self-talk can usually be readily interrupted.

Young people with intellectual disabilities experience visual and auditory hallucinations, and tactile hallucinations appear to be more common (Allington-Smith, 2006). Young people with more severe intellectual disability have difficulty conceptualising and articulating their internal world and may not describe abnormal perceptual experiences. They may appear frightened or perplexed. They do not typically construct a complex secondary delusional system but may express persistent false beliefs, such as a firm belief they are being 'bullied', which, when explored, are not connected to real life experiences. Those who know the young person best often describe 'out of character' behaviour, which has a socially incongruous or disinhibited quality. In the context of enduring psychosis, there is often evidence of increasing and pervasive social withdrawal, with insidious loss of language and cognitive skills. Catatonic features can often be elicited as part of the overall clinical picture, as well as an increase in abnormal movements. Precise sub-classification of psychotic disorders can be difficult to identify precisely in young people with intellectual disability and a focus on the primary features (e.g. the presence of psychotic symptoms or whether psychotic features are persistent and transient) can be a helpful approach in these circumstances. Often, a less discreet onset of symptoms, with a more indolent functional decline, is predicative of a poor long-term outcome.

The onset of psychosis is particularly associated with certain genetic conditions such as Prader-Willi syndrome (Webb *et al*, 2008) and chromosome 22q11.2 deletion syndrome (Swillen *et al*, 2015). The presence of possible seizures either historically or concurrently with the onset of psychotic symptoms should prompt consideration of the psychosis being related to epilepsy e.g. interictal affective psychosis (Toone, 2000). It is particularly important to exclude organic causes of psychosis given the increased rates of intracranial pathology and neurological disorder in young people with intellectual disability.

Mood disorders

Depression can easily be overlooked in young people with intellectual disability. Often, the diagnosis of depression is based on self-report of feelings and ideation. Children and young people with intellectual disability are less likely to assimilate such feelings or describe abstract concepts such as 'feelings of worthlessness' or even 'sadness'. Reports of the non-verbal aspects of depression, such as changes to sleep or appetite, irritability or increased stereotypical or self-injurious behaviour, may be more reliable indicators (Walton, 2016). These may be accompanied by a loss of interest in previously enjoyed activities (anhedonia), social withdrawal or an apparent loss of skills, and the young person may present as 'bored'. Diurnal mood variability can be evident. Sometimes parents or careers may describe 'unhappy' vocalisations in non-verbal young people. The onset of depression may be associated with loss or change in the young person's life, especially with regard to adolescent development and the need for the young person to develop a sense of independence.

Suicidal behaviours may occur, although for young people with severe intellectual disabilities the ability to plan self-harm and suicide, and to act on these plans, is compromised by their level of intellectual functioning (Bernard, 2009).

Like depression, the symptoms of hypomania and mania can be indistinct in children and young people with intellectual disabilities. During adolescence in particular, severe ADHD or autism with marked sensory or emotional dysregulation can mimic hypomania. Certain features of these neurodevelopmental disorders such as impulsivity may become more prominent episodically, and cyclical changes in mood are relatively common in young people with autism in particular, perhaps because small changes in their environment, well-being or lifestyle can trigger changes in their mood. This may represent a variation of cyclothymic disorder (Willem, 2001).

Mania may present with increased motor restlessness, decreased sleep, irritable or elevated mood and aggression (Matson *et al*, 2007). These symptoms may be accompanied by an increase in levels of sexual arousal and behaviour.

Bipolar disorder rarely presents with classic episodes of mania but with episodes of marked psychomotor agitation and altered mood or rapid cycling, where brief occurrences of more obvious depressive or manic states are evident. Often, the young person will return to their 'baseline' state with greater stability of mood and improved functioning.

Case study

Andrew is 15-years-old. He has severe intellectual disability and does not communicate verbally. As a younger child, he loved running in the park or bouncing on a trampoline. He always found it hard to sit still. As he got older, people felt less confident to take Andrew out in public, as he tended to run off when excited.

Over a six-month period, Andrew became increasingly irritable. He seemed bored and frustrated at school. At home, he had started to 'lash out' at his mum. Andrew spent much of his time lying on the sofa. Over a four-week period, Andrew's mum noticed that he no longer made his 'happy noises', laughed less and increasingly made loud, repetitive moaning noises. Andrew stopped using a fork to eat and lost weight. He was reviewed by his Community paediatrician and was physically well apart from a slightly low ferritin level for which he was started on an oral iron supplement. Andrew scored highly on all subscales of the Developmental Behaviour Checklist (DBC).

Andrew had become depressed. A number of precipitating and perpetuating factors were identified. Andrew was missing opportunities for fun and exercise. He was no longer motivated to engage in table-top activities at school. Andrew was started on a low-dose SSRI antidepressant and within a month his mood improved. Andrew was moved to the senior part of the school where a wider range of meaningful activities were available for him. Andrew's social worker arranged for him to join a local swimming group.

Scores on the DBC improved after three months. Andrew's mum reported significant improvements in Andrew's mood and quality life and recognised the importance of him developing new skills and opportunities as he became a young adult.

Anxiety disorders

Children and young people with intellectual disabilities, particularly those with pre-existing ASD, experience high rates of anxiety and anxiety disorder (Cross, 2019). Some studies estimate that up to 84% of young people with ASD have symptoms of anxiety (Vasa, 2015). Almost by definition, children and young people with intellectual disabilities find it harder to make sense of the world around them and to develop effective strategies for negotiating the demands of everyday life. At an intrapsychic and interpersonal level, their feelings and experiences (including bodily tension) are more likely to be experienced as threatening or overwhelming. The anxiety they experience can be 'internalised' or 'externalised' in a variety of ways, such as withdrawal or aggression, and is often under-estimated or misinterpreted. Anxiety may be a pre-cursor of behaviours of concern, which may have an 'escape' function. Anxiety may present as:

■ being 'giddy', fidgety or 'on edge'

■ scanning, checking or repetitive behaviour

■ being overly cautious and reluctant to engage in activities

■ not eating

■ somatic symptoms e.g. sore head

■ self-injurious behaviour.

This predisposition can be explained by a range of biological, psychological and social factors. Children and young people may have genetic conditions associated with anxiety, e.g. Fragile X, or sensory sensitivities which lead to physiological hyperarousal (Burris, 2017). Communication and social interaction difficulties can mean that children and young people with intellectual disabilities are less likely to talk about their fear and worries. Children and young people with intellectual disability experience stressful situations and relationships at home, school and in community settings; they are less likely than their peers to experience acceptance and success and find it difficult to develop positive coping strategies. Low self-esteem and insecure attachment styles may contribute to the development of anxiety disorders (Kurtek, 2016).

Children and young people with intellectual disability experience generalised anxiety, separation anxiety, specific phobias, social anxiety and, less commonly, other forms of anxiety. They are almost five times more likely than their peers to experience separation anxiety (Emerson, 2007) and this may be linked to difficulty sleeping alone or attending school. Selective mutism is also relatively common.

Obsessive-compulsive disorder

Obsessive-compulsive disorder is characterised by the presence of persistent obsessions or compulsions, or most commonly both. It is probably at least as common in children and young people with intellectual disability as the general population (Emerson, 2007), but can be easily missed in individuals with intellectual disability. Children and young people may not be able to conceptualise or report intrusive thoughts or their nature (e.g. whether they experienced ego-dystonic etc.), and compulsions may be misinterpreted as tics or rigid, repetitive behaviours/stereotypies in the context of ASD (Manohar, 2016). It is more likely that those with ASD alone will find the repetitive behaviours soothing, whereas compulsions are experienced as unpleasant because of the associated thoughts such as that they must complete an action until they feel a sense of relief. Trichotillomania may be a feature of OCD. Sexual obsessions have been described in young people with mild intellectual disability (Singh, 2012).

Compulsions can lead to high levels of distress and functional impairment for young people with intellectual disability and large amounts of time may be 'wasted' on the rituals. Cleaning or collecting rituals are among the most commonly seen. Compulsions may be more likely to be associated with changes in physiology and affect than stereotypies, such as irritability or aggression, especially if routines are interrupted. A diagnosis of OCD should be considered based on the behavioural manifestations of the condition even if the classic cognitive symptoms cannot be elicited (Gautam, 2015) because they may respond to specific treatments.

Disorders specifically associated with stress

Children and young people with intellectual disabilities are more likely to be exposed to Adverse Childhood Experiences (ACEs) which have a negative impact on their developmental trajectory and emotional well-being. We know, for example, that they are more likely to be exposed to abuse and the impact of parental mental illness. Attachment- and trauma-related disorders are more likely to be missed in individuals with an intellectual disability (Vervoort-Schel, 2018). There is a growing awareness that children and young people with intellectual disabilities, and especially those with autism, may be exposed to a range of traumatic experiences that are less likely to affect the general population, such as being restrained. It is also the case that they may experience everyday events as traumatic due to misinterpretation of social situations or heightened sensory awareness etc.

The diagnosis of PTSD can follow exposure to an extremely threatening or horrific event such as a road traffic accident. There is also increasing recognition that a wider range of life events may act as catalysts for PTSD in adults with ASD

(Rumball *et al*, 2020). PTSD presents with an internal re-experiencing of the event, avoidance of memories of the event or situations which trigger memories, and an over-perception of threat. Children may be 'watchful' or easily startled, and may report somatic complaints. They may show increased aggression or re-enact the trauma through repetitive play; similar presentations may be seen older adolescents with intellectual disabilities. Repeated exposure to trauma, usually within a specific context from which the individual cannot escape, can lead to complex PTSD. This is characterised by problems with affect regulation, negative self-concept and difficulties sustaining relationships. In young people this can present with dysregulation of affect and behaviour including habitual self-harm. This can be difficult to differentiate from autism spectrum disorder.

The available literature suggests that individuals with intellectual disability are more likely to be exposed to the type of traumatic events which may result in PTSD, that they may be at increased risk of developing PTSD following exposure (due to resilience factors), and that rates of PTSD are higher in this population (Paterson, 2017).

Common presenting features of PTSD in people with intellectual disabilities include sleep disturbance, aggression, self-harm, distractibility, 'jumpiness' and depression (McCarthy, 2001). In young people with intellectual disability, the presentation of PTSD is influenced by the degree and cause of their cognitive impairment, social circumstances, social and communication skills, nature and timing of traumatic experience and subsequent management. PTSD should be considered in any young person with intellectual disabilities who, having experienced serious trauma, presents with changes in their behaviour or emotional state (Turk *et al*, 2005).

Prolonged grief disorders should be considered in young people who have experienced bereavement. They can often be left out of the social rituals surrounding death, or not have death explained to them in a meaningful way, which can lead to an unresolved sense of loss.

Autism spectrum disorder

The prevalence of autism spectrum disorder (ASD) is much higher in children and young people with intellectual disability than the general population; estimates range from 12%-72%, with an average of 34% (Emerson, 2010). Their coexistence their coexistence significantly increases the risk of the child developing mental health or behavioural disorders. 'Kanner-type' autism is associated with an intellectual disability in 70% of cases, but this association drops significantly when broader diagnostic criteria encompassing other autism spectrum conditions are included (Allington-Smith, 2006). Many young people with autism and intellectual disability have significantly impaired or no verbal communication. While ASD can be harder to differentiate from the impairments associated with intellectual disability, especially as the severity of the intellectual disability increases, the *Diagnostic Interview for Social and Communication Disorders* is a valid and helpful tool for use in this population. In those with more severe intellectual disability and ASD, imaginative play is unlikely to be demonstrated. Sensory seeking behaviour, such as approaching people for hugs, may be misinterpreted as sociability.

Children and young people with ASD and intellectual disability will have a unique pattern of strengths and deficits in relation to cognition, communication, sensory modulation and tactile discrimination and motor planning and co-ordination. Levels of self-care and adaptive behaviour will vary significantly according to these and other factors. The presence of intellectual disability in association with ASD increases the risk of self-injury, abnormal fear responses (lack of fear in response to real dangers or excessive fearfulness of everyday events and objects) and problems with eating or drinking, including pica and restricted eating (Kurzius-Spencer 2018).

Increased levels of aggression are commonly seen in young people with ASD and can be related to physical health problems, poor sleep, environmental factors (e.g. noise intolerance), sensory and emotional dysregulation, impaired empathy or cognitive rigidity. Stereotyped aggression may be a form of echopraxia e.g. copied from video games.

Catatonic symptoms can be a feature of ASD in young people with an intellectual disability and should not be overlooked. This includes motor slowness, freezing and maintenance of unusual postures, along with an increase in repetitive movements (Ohta, 2006). The presence of catatonia-like regression should prompt consideration of underlying neurological or psychiatric disorders such as non-convulsive status epilepticus or schizophrenia.

Asperger's syndrome, as a subtype of ASD, is conventionally diagnosed in those with an IQ above 70, and Asperger's original definition emphasised his patients' high intelligence and their acquisition of grammatical speech before they could walk. Nevertheless, some young people who meet the diagnostic criteria for mild intellectual disability and ASD can have a social interaction style, special interests and specific areas of ability which are similar to those of higher ability with a diagnosis of Asperger-type ASD. Pathological Demand Avoidance is disputed as diagnostic sub-type of ASD, however some young people with ASD and intellectual disability display features of demand avoidance with a high level of aversion to social demands and a need to feel in 'control' of social situations to prevent their anxiety becoming intolerable. Recognising these diagnostic subtypes or specific features can be important for developing individualised management strategies.

Many of the genetic syndromes that cause intellectual disability are highly associated with ASD. Increasingly, ASD or ASD-like characteristics have been described in individuals with a range of different genetic syndromes including Tuberous Sclerosis Complex, Fragile X, Cornelia de Lange, Down's, Angelman, Coffin-Lowry, Cohen Laurence-Moon-Biedel, Marinesco-Sjogren, Moebius, Rett and Williams syndromes. The strength of association between these genetic syndromes and ASD is highly variable and the specific manifestation of ASD symptomatology can differ across syndrome groups, with some syndromes showing only certain ASD-like features (Moss, 2012). Children with Fragile X, for example, show impairments related to social anxiety, extreme shyness and eye gaze avoidance (Hall, 2006). Profiles of children with Down's syndrome who meet the screening criteria for ASD show similar profiles of communication and repetitive behaviours to those typically described in autism, however they tend to have relatively milder social difficulties, which may have led to previous assumptions that these conditions did not co-exist. It is important to identify ASD in Down's syndrome due to a greater risk of behavioural disturbance and regression (Warner, 2017).

Attention deficit hyperactivity disorder

Children and young people with intellectual disability are at significantly increased risk of ADHD and as their degree of intellectual impairment increases, the risk for hyperactivity also increases. Studies also suggest that ADHD may have a longer and more persistent course in children with intellectual disability (Xenitidis & Maltezos, 2009).

Attentional problems can be secondary to cognitive impairment, however ADHD should be diagnosed when the child's impairment of attention and activity control is out of proportion to their developmental level. More research is needed to explore the phenomenology of ADHD in intellectual disability, however the evidence that is available offers some reassurance that the psychological characteristics of children with ADHD with and without intellectual disability are similar (Neece, 2011), and that children with intellectual disability with and without high levels of ADHD symptoms show differences in terms of activity behaviours and attention problems (Hastings, 2005).

Comprehensive history taking and observation in a range of settings should attempt to ascertain patterns of inattention with 'flitting and fleeting' activity, higher levels of impulsivity, difficulty waiting, motor over-activity and inability to keep still when seated. For ADHD to be diagnosed, these features should be pervasive across situations and persistent over time (Royal College of Psychiatrists, 2001). The Developmental Behaviour Checklist (DBC) was developed on, and standardised for, populations of children and adolescents with intellectual disability and the hyperactivity subscale contains six items with face validity for ADHD. The Conner's Childhood Behaviour Rating Scale can also be helpful. Such scales should indicate the presence of the ADHD symptom complex and can provide a pre-treatment baseline measure. Children with ADHD have problems with working memory or motor inhibition that are 'above and beyond' their degree of general impairment.

There are a number of conditions which are highly associated with ADHD and where the diagnosis should specifically be considered. These include:

- Genetic e.g. Fragile X, Angelman
- Mucopolysaccharidoses (Hunters etc.)
- Neurocutaneous disorders (Neurofibromatosis, tuberous sclerosis)
- Post brain injury/insult (e.g. RTA, meningitis)
- Epilepsy syndromes: Dravet; Lennox-Gastaut.

There are a number of physical, developmental and mental health conditions which can mimic the presentation of ADHD, as can the effects of some medications. It is important to identify and manage these before considering the diagnosis of ADHD, especially for physical health problems which require treatment such as sleep apnoea or anaemia. Tics can be mistaken for over-activity and their presence should be clearly established before diagnosing and treating ADHD.

Case study

Mary is eight years old. She lives with her parents and younger brother. Mary has Dravet syndrome. She is non-verbal. Mary's teachers have reported that she spends much of her time in school climbing over furniture. While she occasionally shows interest in activities, this is momentary. During group-based activities Mary will throw things at other children. Mary's parents were exhausted and reported that they were 'unable to take their eyes off Mary, even for a second'.

Mary was referred to ID CAMHS who considered possible ADHD. Mary's seizures were well controlled on valproate and her parents felt that her concentration had improved slightly with improved seizure control. A Conner's CBRS was completed as a baseline measure, and Mary was 'off the scale' on measures of hyperactivity for her chronological age. The team arranged for Mary to wear a pedometer, which was showed she was walking over 15,000 steps per day. A comprehensive assessment concluded that Mary had ADHD. Mary had an ECG before pharmacological treatment was considered, given the association between Dravet syndrome and long QT syndrome.

Tic disorders

Children and young people with intellectual disabilities are more likely than their typically developing peers to experience the full spectrum of tic disorders, from self-limiting simple tics to severe Tourette's. The 11th revision of the International Classification of Diseases (ICD-11) describes a subtype of tic disorder (secondary tics) as 'a direct consequence of a neurodevelopmental disorder'.

Tics can be difficult to distinguish from stereotyped or ritualistic behaviour associated with the young person's underlying neurodevelopmental disorder or possible OCD symptoms (rituals and compulsions), and indeed these symptoms may co-exist (Wolicki et al, 2019). Stereotypies are seen in both severe intellectual disability and ASD, and co-occurring facial grimacing can contribute to diagnostic confusion (Freeman et al, 2010).

Severe, complex motor tics may have an apparent sudden onset in late childhood or early adolescence, although simple tics will often have been overlooked in earlier years.

Most young people with intellectual disability experiencing tics will not describe a classic 'premonitory urge', although a degree of dysphoria may be evident to a skilled observer prior to a tic or burst of tics. Tics may be exacerbated by boredom or stress. Explosive, tic-like aggression can be seen in young people with severe tic disorders.

It is important to establish to what extent tics might cause the child pain or distress, or interrupt their functioning. It is important to consider whether severe motor tics might particularly compromise a young person with musculoskeletal abnormalities.

Sleep disorders

Sleep problems are extremely common in children with intellectual disabilities (MacCrosain & Byrne, 2009). They are associated with increased emotional and behavioural difficulties, including irritability and hyperactivity (Valicenti-McDermott et al, 2019) and impact the child's cognitive function.

Children can have difficulty settling to sleep or maintaining sleep. Parents describe frequent night-time wakening or reduced sleep duration, sometimes with the child wakening apparently refreshed after a relatively short amount of sleep. This may be associated with anxieties about sleeping alone. It is useful to establish whether the child has ever achieved the key developmental task of being able to self-soothe and settle to sleep alone.

Sleep deprivation and increased stress can impact parents and sibling's well-being, as well as family relationships.

It is critical to consider and exclude medical conditions such as nocturnal seizures, sleep apnoea or gastroesophageal reflux, especially when these are known to be associated with a particular genetic diagnosis affecting the child. Sleep-disordered breathing and obstructive sleep apnoea is common in children with Down's syndrome. Pain can disrupt sleep in children with intellectual disability, even if the child is taking medication to reduce pain (Breau & Camfield, 2011).

Sleep disorders may also represent a co-morbidity, especially ADHD, or the onset of an anxiety or mood disorder.

Behaviour disorders or behaviours of concern

Various conceptual frameworks or classification systems exist to describe persistent patterns of behaviour which require assessment and intervention, either because they impact significantly on the young person's quality of life and social functioning or are associated with a risk of harm to themselves or others e.g. aggressive behaviour. These include the descriptor of 'challenging behaviour', as well as the diagnosis of 'conduct disorder'. When assessing behaviours of concern or conduct problems, the nature and extent of the child or young person's developmental difficulties should be considered.

The concept of challenging behaviour was developed in 1995 as a descriptive term to highlight the need for behaviour analysis and resultant intervention. It was defined as 'culturally abnormal behaviour(s) of such an intensity, frequency or duration that the physical safety of the person or others is likely to be placed in serious jeopardy, or behaviour which is likely to seriously limit the use of, or result in a person being denied access to, ordinary community facilities' (Emerson, 2001). Challenging behaviour should not be used as a diagnostic term. Recent research has implicated a wide-range of underlying disorders including ADHD, anxiety and depression, alongside sub-diagnostic traits such as poor impulse control and stereotyped behaviours.

The diagnosis of conduct disorder depends on a repetitive and persistent pattern of behaviour in which the basic rights of others or major age-appropriate societal rules are violated to a sufficient extent that important areas of functioning are impaired. This is the most common diagnosis among children and adolescents with intellectual disabilities (Emerson, 2003). With regard to the diagnostic criteria for conduct disorder, it should be acknowledged that a young person with intellectual disability cannot be expected to understand rules to the same extent as their age peers. It is more helpful to consider the behaviour as an indicator of some form unmet need in relation to the young person's adaptive functioning, such as the need for a shared communication system or increased predictability in day-to-day routines.

Behaviours of concern and conduct problems should be considered as the external manifestations of a wide range of possible underlying problems, rather than a single entity (Rathwell & Simonoff, 2019). When a child or young person presents with behaviours of concern or conduct disorder, biological as well as psychological factors should be considered as predisposing, precipitating and perpetuating factors.

Biological factors may be linked to the child's genetic condition or underlying physical health problems. Behavioural phenotypes are being described for an increasing number of genetic conditions. Knowledge of behavioural phenotypes allows an earlier, preventative approach to predictable patterns of behaviour e.g. increased repetitive behaviour and social anxiety in Fragile X syndrome (Mijovic & Turk, 2008). It is important to ensure recognition and optimal management of underlying physical health conditions, as symptoms such as pain or post-seizure disorientation can manifest behaviourally (Turk *et al*, 2009).

The concept of 'diagnostic overshadowing' emphasises that behaviours of concern can be assumed to be an inherent part of an individual's intellectual disability, rather than a mental health condition, to such extent that symptoms such as underlying low mood can go unrecognised (Hayes *et al*, 2011). Sub-diagnostic psychological traits, such as impulsivity or a predisposition to stereotyped behaviour, may also predispose the individual to increased rates of challenging behaviour or conduct disorder. Recognising core symptoms or symptom complexes may be specific targets for intervention.

Taking these factors into account, the function of the behaviour should be assessed in terms of how the child has learned to negotiate environmental challenges by gaining something experienced as rewarding, for example parental attention, or avoiding something experienced as aversive such as non-preferred activities. Children and young people with social anxiety, for example, may develop a repertoire of behaviours which serve the function of avoiding social demands. In this case, strategies to help the child understand the social situation and develop their social skills can be used alongside specific evidence-based interventions for anxiety. Additionally, the type of temper tantrums typically displayed in most two-year-old children may persist for longer in children with intellectual disability (Allington-Smith, 2006) and the importance of early intervention to prevent maladaptive patterns of behaviour becoming established is increasingly understood (Guralnick, 2011).

The key message is that when children and young people with intellectual disabilities begin to show patterns of behaviour that impact on their quality of life and social functioning, or are associated with a risk of harm to themselves or others, a comprehensive assessment leading to an individualised intervention plan should be undertaken (NICE, 2015).

Conclusion

Children and young people with intellectual disability are more likely to experience mental health conditions or emotional and behavioural difficulties than their typically developing peers. These conditions present differently depending on the child's developmental and intellectual functioning and the potential co-existence of several conditions. Recognising such difficulties, and ensuring timely access to therapeutic supports and evidence-based interventions, are key to improving the child's developmental trajectory and quality of life.

It is imperative that all those working with children and young people with intellectual difficulties have an awareness of mental health issues, and that children and young people can access specialist services who have the expertise and resources available to recognise and treat the full range of mental health conditions, neurodevelopmental disorders and emotional difficulties they experience. Often this requires careful interpretation of subtle changes in the young person's behaviour and consideration of biological, psychological and social factors which may be important in the diagnostic formulation. Given that children and young people are often unable to self-report, collaborative history taking and structured observation are particularly important.

An increased focus on access to evidence-based interventions and improved quality of life will lead to better outcomes for children and young people and their families.

References

Allington-Smith P (2006) Mental health of children with intellectual disabilities. *Advances in Psychiatric Treatment* **12** 130–140.

Aman H, Naeem F, Farooq S & Ayub M (2016) Prevalence of nonaffective psychosis in intellectually disabled clients: systematic review and meta-analysis. *Psychiatric Genetics* **26** (4) 145–155.

Bernard S (2009) Mental health and behavioural problems in children and adolescents with intellectual disabilities. *Psychiatry* 387–390.

Breau LM & Camfield CS (2011) Pain disrupts sleep in children and youth with intellectual and developmental disabilities. *Research in Developmental Disabilities* **32** 2829–2840.

Burris JL, Barry-Anwar RA, Sims RN, Hagerman RJ, Tassone F & Rivera SM (2017) Children with Fragile X Syndrome display threat-specific biases towards emotion. *Biological Psychiatry: Cognitive Neuroscience and neuroimaging* **2** (6) 487–492.

Clarke DJ, Boer H, Whittington J, Holland A, Butler J & Webb T (2002) Prader-Willi Syndrome, compulsive and ritualistic behaviours: the first population based survey. *British Journal of Psychiatry* **180** 358–362.

Corbett J (1977) Studies of mental retardation. In: PJ Graham (Ed) *Epidemiological Approaches in Child Psychiatry*. London: Academic Press.

Crawford H, Waite J & Oliver C (2017) Diverse profiles of anxiety related disorders in Fragile X, Cornelia de Lange and Rubenstein-Taybi Syndromes. *Journal of Autism and Developmental Disorders* **43** 3728–3740.

Cross AJ, Goharpey N, Laycock R & Gillard-Crewther S (2019) Anxiety as a common biomarker for school children with additional health and development needs irrespective of diagnosis. *Frontiers in Psychology* Available at: https://doi.org/10.3389/fpsyg.2019.01420 (accessed June 2020).

Einfeld SL & Tonge BJ (1996) Population prevalence of psychopathology in children and adolescents with intellectual disability: II epidemiological findings. *Journal of Intellectual Disability Research* **40** (2) 91–98.

Emerson E (2001) *Challenging Behaviour: Analysis and intervention in people with intellectual disabilities 2nd Edition*. Cambridge University Press.

Emerson E (2003) Prevalence of psychiatric disorders in children and adolescents without and without intellectual disability. *Journal of Intellectual Disability Research* **47** 51–58.

Emerson E & Baines S (2010) *The Estimated Prevalence of Autism among Adults with Learning Disabilities in England. Improving Health and Lives: Learning Disabilities Observatory*.

Emerson E & Hatton C (2007) Mental health of children and adolescents with intellectual disabilities in Britain. *British Journal of Psychiatry* **191** (6) 493–499.

Freeman RD, Soltanifar A & Baer S (2010) Stereotypic movement disorder: easily missed. *Developmental Medicine and Child Neurology* **52** (8) 733–738.

Gautam P & Bhatia MS (2015) Obsessive Compulsive Disorder with Intellectual Disability: a diagnostic and therapeutic challenge. *Journal of Clinical and Diagnostic Research* 9 1–2.

Guralnick M (2011) Why early intervention works: a systemic perspective. *Infants Young Child* 24(1) 6-28.

Hall S, deBernardis M & Reiss A (2006) Social Escape Behaviours in Individuals with Fragile X Syndrome. *Journal of Autism and Developmental Disorders* **36** 935–947.

Hastings RP, Beck A, Daley D & Hill C (2005) Symptoms of ADHD and their correlates in children with intellectual disabilities. *Research in Developmental Disabilities* **26** 456–468.

Hayes S, McGuire B, O'Neill M, Oliver C & Morrison T (2011) Low mood and challenging behaviour in people with severe and profound intellectual disabilities. *Journal of Intellectual Disability Research* **55** (2) 182–189.

Kurtek P (2016) Role of anxiety as a trait and state in youth with mild intellectual disability: coping with difficult situations. *Journal of Policy and Practice in Intellectual Disabilities* **13** (3) 236–245.

Kurzius-Spencer M, Pettygrove S, Christensen D, Pedersen AL, Cunniff C, Maeney J, Soke GN, Harrington RA, Durkin M & Rice S (2018) Behavioural problems in children with and without co-occurring intellectual disability. *Research in Autism Spectrum Disorders* **56** 61–71.

MacCrosain AM & Byrne MC (2009) Are we ignoring the problem of sleep disorder in children with intellectual disabilities? *Irish Journal of Medical Science* **178** (4) 427–431.

Matson J, González ML, Terlonge C, Thorson RT, Laud RB (2007) What symptoms predict the diagnosis of mania in persons with severe/profound intellectual disability in clinical practice? *Journal of Intellectual Disability Research* **51**(1) 25-31

Manohar H, Subramanian K, Kandasamy P, Penchilaiya V & Arun A (2016) Diagnostic masking and overshadowing – how structured evaluation helps. *Journal of Child and Adolescent Psychiatric Nursing* **29** 171–176.

McCarthy J (2001) Post-traumatic stress disorder in people with intellectual disability. *Advances in Psychiatric Treatment* **7** 163–169.

Mijovic A & Turk J (2008) Behavioural phenotypes and child and adolescent mental health. *Current Medical Literature Paediatrics* **21** 1–9.

Moss J & Oliver C (2012) *Autism in genetic syndromes: Implications for assessment and intervention. Cerebra Centre for Neurodevelopmental Disorders* [online]. Available at: www.findresources.co.uk (accessed June 2020).

NICE (2015) *Challenging behaviour and intellectual disabilities: prevention and interventions for people with intellectual disabilities whose behaviour challenges* [online]. Available at: www.nice.org.uk/guidance/ng11 (accessed June 2020).

Neece CL, Baker BL, Blacher J & Crnic KA (2011) Attention deficit/hyperactivity disorder among children with and without intellectual disability: an examination across time. *Journal of Intellectual Disability Research* **55** (7) 623–635.

Ohta M, Kano Y & Nagai Y (2006) Catatonia in individuals with Autism Spectrum Disorders in adolescence and early adulthood: a long-term prospective study. *International Review of Neurobiology* **72** 41–54.

Paterson B, Young J & Bradley P (2017) Recognising and responding to trauma in the implementation of PBS? *BILD: International Journal of Positive Behaviour Support* **7** (1) 4–14.

Royal College of Psychiatrists (2001) *DC-LD: Diagnostic criteria for psychiatric disorders for use with adults with intellectual disabilities/mental retardation.* Occasional paper OP48. London: Gaskell.

Rathwell R & Simonoff E (2019) Editorial perspective: Key issues in children with intellectual disability for practitioners. *Child and Adolescent Mental health* **24** (2) 194–198.

Rumball F, Happe F & Grey N (2020) Experience of Trauma and PTSD Symptoms in Autistic Adults: Risk of PTSD Development Following DSM -5 and Non-DSM -5 Traumatic Life Events. *Autism Research.* Available at: https://doi.org/10.1002/aur.2306 (accessed April 2020).

Singh G & Coffey BJ (2012) Sexual obsessions, compulsions, suicidality and homicidality in an adolescent diagnosed with bipolar disorder not otherwise specified, obsessive-compulsive disorder, pervasive developmental disorder not otherwise specified, and mild mental retardation. *Journal Of Child And Adolescent Psychopharmacology* **22** 250–3.

Swillen A & McDonald-McGinn D (2015) Developmental trajectories in 22q11.2 deletion syndrome. *American Journal of Medical Genetics – C.* **189** (2) 172–181.

Toone B (2000) The psychoses of epilepsy. *Journal of Neurology, Neurosurgery and Psychiatry* **69** 1–3.

Turk J, Bax M, Williams C, Amin P, Eriksson M, Gilberg, C (2009) Autism spectrum disorder in children with and without epilepsy: Impact on social functioning and communication. *Acta Peadiatrica, International Journal of Peadiatrics* **98**: 675 - 681

Turk J, Robbins I & Woodhead M (2005) Post Traumatic Stress Disorder in Young People with Intellectual Disability. *Journal of Intellectual Disability Research* **49** (11) 872–875.

Valicenti-McDermott M, Lawson K, Hottinger K, Seijo R, Schechtman M, Shulman L & Shinnar S (2019) Sleep problems in children with autism and other developmental disabilities: a brief report. *Journal of Child Neurology* **34** (7) 387–393.

Vasa RA & Mazurek MO (2016) An update on anxiety in youth with autism spectrum disorders. *Current Opinion in Psychiatry* **28** (2) 83–90.

Vervoort-Schel J, Mercera G, Wissink I, Mink E, Van der Helm P, Lindauer R & Moonen X (2018) Adverse Childhood Experiences in Children with Intellectual Disabilities: An Exploratory Case-File Study in Dutch Residential Care. *International Journal of Environmental Research and Public Health* **15** (10) 2136.

Walton C & Kerr M (2016) Severe intellectual disability: systematic review of the prevalence and nature of presentation of unipolar depression. *Journal of Applied Research in Intellectual Disabilities* **29** (5) 395–408.

Warner G, Howlin P, Salamone E, Moss J & Charman T (2017) Profiles of children with Down Syndrome who meet screening criteria for autism spectrum disorder (ASD): a comparison with children diagnosed with ASD attending special schools. *Journal of Intellectual Disability Research* **61** (1) 75–82.

Webb T, Mania EN, Soni S, Whittington J, Boer H, Clarke D & Holland A (2008) In search of psychosis gene in people with Prader-Willi syndrome. *American Journal of Medical Genetics* **146** (7) 843–853.

Willem MA, Tuinier S (2001) Cyclothymia or unstable mood disorder? A systematic treatment evaluation with valproic acid. *Journal of Applied Research in Intellectual Disabilities* **14** 147–154.

Wolicki SB, Bitsko RH, Danielson ML, Holbrook JR, Zablotsky B, Walkup JT, Woods DW & Mink JW (2019) Children with Tourette syndrome in the United States: parent-reported diagnosis, co-occurring disorders, severity and influence of activities on tics. *Journal of Developmental and Behavioral Pediatrics* **40** (6) 407–414.

Xenitidis K & Maltezos S (2009) Attention deficit hyperactivity disorder in adults with intellectual disabilities. *Psychiatry* **8** 402–404.

Chapter 5: Psychological assessment

Dr Suzannah Gratton

Chapter summary

Psychologists can take many roles when working with young people with intellectual disabilities and their families. Some of these are unique to clinical psychologists while others may be shared with a range of mental health and neurodevelopmental specialists. Assessment of difficulties with behaviour and a range of intervention approaches are considered elsewhere in this book, and so the present chapter attempts to consider roles that are largely unique to psychologists: cognitive or neuropsychological assessment, thinking especially of how this contributes to the identification and diagnosis of intellectual disability and assessment with a view to psychological formulation of mental health and/or behaviour problems. General skills connected to engaging children, administering, scoring and interpreting assessments are covered in other texts. This chapter focuses on the range of tests available and approaches to assessment.

Tools for assessment

An ever-increasing number of psychological tests and rating scales are available to both identify intellectual disability and to contribute to the assessment of behaviour and mental health problems in intellectual disability. When tools are well constructed and psychometrically robust they are able to support the collection of objective data on functioning over time and should support greater consensus between clinicians. The quality of a tool is judged by its psychometric properties (Carr, 2006):

- Reliability – the degree to which the outcome can be consistently repeated.

- Validity – the extent to which the tool measures the construct it purports to measure.

- Standardisation – the degree to which the administration and scoring procedures are objective and replicable and that the test is calibrated against 'norms' established by using a large and representative sample of individuals.

Often very few people with intellectual disability are included in standardisation samples, which may impact on validity.

■ User friendliness – features that make the test engaging to clients and easy to administer.

Test publishing companies restrict the use and purchase of many assessment tools to HCPC-registered practitioner psychologists and others with test-specific appropriate qualifications. It is important that the most recently standardised versions of the test are used to ensure that results are not affected by the Flynn Effect (Flynn, 1987) and so report an inflated IQ.

Assessment of intellectual ability

A significant impairment in intellectual ability is a key part of diagnosis, although emphasis in recent iterations of diagnostic systems has shifted away from focus on the IQ score to whether the individual's everyday functioning is impaired. Hence, an IQ score is still useful but it is not the only criteria by which decisions about diagnosis and access to services should be made. Current diagnostic criteria are discussed in Chapter 2 of this book. The most widely used assessments are the Wechsler tests, which in their different forms will assess typically developing children from two and a half years into adulthood. They aim to provide information about areas of cognitive functioning such as verbal comprehension, visual-spatial and fluid reasons (sometimes known as non-verbal or perceptual reasoning), working memory and processing speed, as well as an indication of overall cognitive ability reported by the Full Scale IQ Score. Each assessment also allows for a more detailed profile of performance across the different domains of functioning. Alternatives to the Wechsler tests include the *British Ability Scales: Third Edition* and the *Kaufman Assessment Battery for Children: Second Edition*.

Assessments that measure IQ and so identify intellectual disability, do so by recording where an individual's performance lies on the continuum of ability of people of the same age in the population, where ability is assumed to be normally distributed. This means that a large range of scores is in the 'average range' and so at the level expected for that age. Conventionally, scores within 1 standard deviation of the mean are considered 'average' while 2 standard deviations below the mean constitutes an impairment. The Wechsler tests give standard scores with a mean of 100 and a standard deviation of 15. Hence a score of under 70 is consistent with a intellectual disability.

In this context, it is also worth explaining that health and education can use different diagnostic criteria and terminology, yet professionals and parents are often not aware of this and use terms interchangeably. Intellectual *disability* is health terminology, while education terminology is learning *difficulties*, and the categories for mild, moderate and severe levels of impairment do not coincide (see Table 5.1). For the sake of clarity, it can be helpful to specify both terms in reports when relevant.

Table 5.1: Classification of IQ in health & education

IQ range	Health (ICD-10) Intellectual *disability*	IQ range	Education learning *difficulty*
50-69	Mild	55-69	Moderate
35-49	Moderate	<55	Severe
20-34	Severe		
<20	Profound	<20	Profound & multiple

Assessing pre-school children

Where concerns about development are raised very early on, this is usually owing to a failure to attain specific developmental milestones by a particular point. In very young children, early development is uneven and the rate and timing at which new skills emerge varies significantly between children. Hence there is a large range of what constitute normal development. Development begins with sensory systems and early functional skills, and these change over time. Cognitive skills of memory, language and attention are relatively undifferentiated at first but as children mature higher cognitive domains emerge including verbal and spatial reasoning, working memory, inhibition, long-term memory and language, which can then be measured.

Assessment of development in infancy focuses on observable skills and makes a judgement about whether this skill is typically shown by a child of this age. Tools that assess developmental level usually report an age-equivalent and so identify the amount of 'delay' a child is showing at any point in time. Alternatively, they report a developmental quotient, which give the child's development as a proportion of what is 'typical' for someone of that age. Performance of 2 standard deviations below the mean, or a 25% delay in age-equivalents, is considered a significant delay. Issues with this approach are that it supposes there is a typical child, where as in fact all children have slightly different paths of development, and reporting impairments in terms of a particular amount of delay is problematic because its significance varies depending on the age of the child e.g. a delay of three months at six months old is far more significant than a delay of three months at three years old. Hence it is problematic to measure change.

Because early development is uneven, DQs or age-equivalent, it is not a good predictor of long-term outcomes. It is also the case that, for some parents, the term 'delay' implies that their child will eventually catch-up with their peers. Yet once a child is out of the pre-school years and their development is still significantly behind their age peers, catching up becomes less likely. For these reasons developmental assessments are very useful for identifying early difficulties and giving snapshots of abilities at particular points, but once a child is old enough for measures of intellectual ability and adaptive functioning they should be reassessed and diagnoses of developmental delay moved on to ones of intellectual disability, if appropriate.

Common developmental assessment tools include the Bayley Scales of Early Development, the Griffiths Mental Development Scales and the Mullen Scales of Early Learning. These assessments are usually carried out with a parent present and are suitable from birth into the preschool years, with the Bayley going to 42 months and Mullen and Griffiths assessments going to 68 months and 72 months respectively.

Once a child is aged two and a half, the Wechsler Pre-School and Primary Scale of Intelligence (WPPSI-IV) can be used, and this is a measure of intelligence rather than development. For children aged from two years six months to three years 11 months the WPPSI-IV assesses verbal comprehension, visual spatial ability and working memory as part of the Full Scale IQ. It can also be used to assess early vocabulary acquisition. In this way a more limited but developmentally appropriate range of cognitive abilities are tested than the WPPSI measures for older children. In the pre-school years, once a child is out of infancy, assessment of IQ with the WPPSI-IV is preferable to developmental assessments where possible but reassessment when older is likely to be needed as cognitive development is still uneven and the results lack predictive validity until around age seven (McCall, 1977).

Testing school-age children

By far the most widely used assessments of intellectual ability are the Wechsler tests. The Wechsler Pre-School and Primary Scale of Intelligence Fourth Edition (WPPSI-IV) is suitable for children aged two years and six months to seven years, seven months, while the Wechsler Intelligence Scale for Children-Fifth Edition (WISC-V) can be used with those aged six years to 16 years, 11 months. Both of these measures report on verbal comprehension, visual-spatial and fluid reasons, working memory and processing speed as giving a Full Scale IQ Score. If the child is in the overlap between the two assessments then it is better to use the WPPSI-V as this will be more accessible to the child and has a lower floor. These take 60 to 90 minutes to administer and can be carried out over multiple sessions if needed. Over the age of 16, the Wechsler Adult Intelligence Scale-Fourth Edition is used.

As children develop, so the range of cognitive abilities they show enlarges and these can also be quantified through formal assessment. Specific tools are available to assess neuropsychological functions including memory, executive functioning, attention, language and visuo-spatial processing. These assessments of more complex neuropsychological functions are generally not suitable for young people with moderate to severe intellectual disability but may add to the understanding of how to support someone with a mild intellectual disability if they appear to be struggling in specific areas in a way that is thought to be out of keeping with their overall level of development. However, there should always be a specific hypothesis to investigate rather than using them as a routine part of assessment. An alternative approach to assessment is to use the Wechsler Individual Attainment Test-Third Edition (WIAT-III), which assesses academic attainment as opposed to intellectual ability in four to 25 year olds. This can be useful when there are concerns that there is a mismatch between intellectual ability and performance at school, but it is only appropriate for those with mild learning difficulties who have some basic literacy and numeracy skills.

Assessing young people with limited spoken English

Sometimes it is necessary to try to assess the cognitive abilities of young people with limited spoken English. Two common scenarios for this are when a young person has only recently started to learn English or when it is suspected that someone's non-verbal intellectual abilities are very much stronger than their verbal ones, as can occasionally be the case for people with autistic spectrum disorder. There are a number of options in this scenario. If the young person is over the age of seven and reported to speak relatively well in their first language, then a subsection of the WISC-V subtests can be used to calculate the Nonverbal Index, which can be used to give an indication of someone's intellectual ability. An alternative is the Raven's Colour Progressive Matrices, which is non-verbal. For the general population, scores on the Raven's and earlier versions for the WISC have been strongly correlated. However, it may be that young people with a diagnosis of autism will score more highly on the Ravens than the WISC and so results should be interpreted cautiously (Nader *et al*, 2016) probably owing to the narrow range of cognitive abilities assessed by the Ravens. The final option is the Leiter International Performance Scales, 3rd Edition (Leiter-3), which assesses a range of non-verbal abilities. This is a less common assessment tool although it has long history of use in services for people with intellectual disability. The advantages of the Leiter-3 are that it can be used from three years upwards and that the instructions as well as the responses are non-verbal and so it overcomes some of the difficulties with receptive as well as expressive language.

Assessing children and young people with severe intellectual disabilities

For children whose language is limited and who have clear significant impairments in daily living skills compared to their age peers, cognitive assessments may not be needed to diagnose a intellectual disability. However, there are situations where it is helpful to try to get a clearer understanding of a young person's abilities. This is especially true when there are concerns that carers are overestimating someone's abilities and so unrealistic expectations are contributing to behaviour difficulties, when inadequate levels of support are being provided or when there are queries about the most appropriate treatment approaches. Most intelligence tests have a floor of IQ 40 and can reliably distinguish mild and moderate intellectual disability, but not between severe and profound levels of impairment. For young people with severe difficulties a standardised assessment using an age-appropriate tool will simply identify that the young person is functioning below the floor of the assessment. The process of testing is also likely to be frustrating and difficult for them to engage in as they are being asked to do tasks that they are unable to understand or do. This not usually a constructive approach.

A guide to the level of cognitive development can be obtained by using an assessment designed for younger children and calculating the age-equivalent using the raw scores and the appropriate table in the manual. If helpful, these can then be interpreted as a proportion of chronological age. For instance, the WPPSI-IV or the Mullen could be used to gather age-equivalent scores depending on the estimated developmental level of the young person. However, there are many cautions to this approach and the list below starts with the most important:

■ An age-equivalent can be easily misinterpreted as meaning that the young person is 'as a child of that age'. However, the life experiences, interests, aspirations and expectations of the young person are very different and in many areas will far exceed their age-equivalent score.

■ It is not possible to say how significant or unusual the differences between scores are and so any comments about the nature of the cognitive profile or differences between skill areas need to be made very cautiously.

■ The detailed nature of age-equivalent scores in months and years can give a false sense of certainty about the level of functioning. It is more appropriate for them to be used as a guide, viewed in broad ranges, rather than a detailed reflection of level of functioning.

■ Age equivalents can also imply that a child with a chronological age of, for example, 10, and age-equivalent of five, is the same as a child who has a chronological and developmental age of five. This is misleading because for many children their development is not merely delayed but follows a different trajectory, and so they may be using different cognitive strategies to achieve the same outcome as a typically developing child.

Assessment of adaptive functioning

Adaptive functioning refers to performance in the range of skills that are necessary to manage the demands of everyday life effectively. These will vary depending on the environment around the person. The Diagnostic and Statistical Manual of mental Disorders, Fourth Edition (DSM-IV) considers the key areas that must be taken into account to be:

- communication
- community use
- functional academics
- school/home living
- health and safety
- leisure
- self-care
- self-direction
- social work (for older adolescents or adults only).

While a general impression of abilities in these areas can be gathered through observation or interviewing those involved in supporting the young person, assessment measures have been developed that quantify abilities and plot them along a normal distribution so enabling significant impairments to be identified. Commonly used measures are the Adaptive Behaviour Assessment System, Third Edition (ABAS-3), and the Vineland Adaptive Behaviour Scales-3. As well as contributing to diagnosis, adaptive functioning is also useful both for being aware of support needs and for planning interventions to improve independent living skills, which are especially important for those approaching adulthood.

The ABAS-3 uses report forms that are suitable from birth to age 89 years. There are separate forms for parents/carers and teachers/day care which are also separated by age groups: 0-5 years, 5-21 years and adult. The forms are quite long, taking at least 20 minutes to complete, and require a reasonable level of literacy in the person completing. They were developed in America and some of the terminology requires adaptation for the UK. Once the scoring criteria have been explained, the form is relatively straightforward as all items are completed. The form for the correct age group should be completed. However, for very low functioning children this has the same problem as standardised IQ tests in that it will just identify that they are working below the level of the floor of the assessment. In these situations, the 0-5 age form can be used and age-equivalents calculated but all the cautions already outlined for using age-equivalents apply. The domains of the ABAS-3 match the domains of the DSM-IV criteria for intellectual disability and the form allows summary scores to be calculated for the skill areas of conceptual, social and practical as well as a summary General Ability Composite score.

The Vineland-3 covers the age range of birth to 90 years and is available as a report form for parents/carers or teachers, or as an interview administered by a clinician, and there is a comprehensive version and an abbreviated, domain level version of each form, although the domain level form is only suitable for age three and over. The comprehensive form uses basal and ceiling rules so that not all items need to be completed, however parents and carers can find this difficult to put into practice on the report form. Domain level scores for communication, daily living and socialisation can be calculated, as well as an overall summary score.

Formulation

Once the tests have been administered, scored and interpreted as directed in the manual, the results also need to be interpreted in light of information gained through observing the young person during the assessment and through clinical interviews.

It is necessary to consider whether the test scores reflect 'true' ability within the margin of error (confidence intervals) or whether they were significantly influenced by historical or contextual factors such as marked deprivation, abuse, very chaotic home situations, physical or sensory impairments or mental health issues. Test results can also be significantly affected by engagement and effort, the use of strategies or anxiety, and these need to be taken into account when interpreting the results. This contextual information is very important and test scores should never be taken in isolation.

Once the meaning of the scores has been determined, one of the main functions of this information will be to determine whether a diagnosis of intellectual disability is relevant. When test results are at diagnostic boundaries, especially when the confidence interval includes 70, clinical judgement must exercised both in taking account of context and considering the possible impact of a decision about diagnosis on access to services, the effect on the network and on the child's identity.

Cognitive assessment information will also be helpful in contributing to whether additional diagnoses should be made, for instance considering whether a child's level of activity is out of keeping with their approximate developmental age. Integration with information from school can help to understand whether a child is achieving as expected and recommendations could be made to support the child at school both behaviourally and academically. Cognitive or neuropsychological assessments should always lead to recommendations to improve functioning rather than being an end in themselves. Recommendations often cover areas such as the features of school provision that will meet the young person's needs and strategies to maximise concentration, memory and learning at home and school.

IQ and level of functioning information should also be used to help add context to a young person's presenting difficulties. For instance, identified low IQ is likely to be a significant contributor to behavioural difficulties at school if the young person is frustrated at not being able to understand lessons or has found that being disruptive is an effective way of getting out of lessons that they do not understand. Similarly, carers or school staff overestimating a young person's abilities and so having expectations that the young person is not developmentally able to meet is also likely to be a significant contributor to mental health and behaviour difficulties.

A final area where a good understanding of a young person's intellectual abilities is very helpful is to inform what treatment approaches are likely to be appropriate. Evidence based individual therapeutic approaches such as CBT for anxiety or depression, even when highly adapted, require sufficient language and cognitive ability to report on events and internal experiences and recognise that others may hold different perspectives (Jahoda, 2016). When a young person has a low level of functioning then both behavioural and mental health difficulties are more appropriately managed through modifying the environment, aiming to improve quality of life, teaching skills and providing functional alternatives using a positive behavioural support framework (Gore *et al*, 2013).

Conclusions

Psychologists have unique skills in the assessment of cognitive and neuropsychological functioning. Understanding intellectual ability and adaptive functioning are central to diagnosis of intellectual disability and formal assessment is especially important for those whose impairment is not immediately obvious. Standardised assessment tools are available that will reliably identify when someone's IQ is below 70 and can successfully differentiate between mild and moderate levels of intellectual disability. The most commonly used tools have a floor of 40 and so are not able to differentiate between severe and profound intellectual disabilities. When it is apparent that a young person has an intellectual disability, there can still sometimes be a benefit in carrying out a cognitive assessment using an assessment tool standardised for younger children and then reporting age-equivalent scores. However, the results of this must be interpreted very cautiously and the limitations communicated clearly. Cognitive and adaptive functioning information should always lead to an understanding of a young person's strengths and support needs, and the information should contribute to a wider formulation of their presenting difficulties such as allowing behaviour to be understood in its developmental context or in considering whether the child is able to meet the demands and expectations the system places on them.

Case vignette

Oliver is a nine-year-old boy who was referred for assessment and management of physical and verbal aggression, which was often related to being unable to engage in his significant obsessions. Oliver attended a special school which catered for those with severe learning difficulties, in educational terminology, and they had noted that while his spoken language was fluent, his attainment on school-like tasks was at the pre-school level. On meeting Oliver, his verbal fluency was striking and felt to be at odds with his school attainment and there were questions over whether he would be able to access some very simplified individual psychological intervention or whether the focus should be on environmental modification and behavioural work with his parents. To help clarify the nature of his learning difficulties and possible interventions, a cognitive assessment was completed.

The assessment strategy was to collate information about his attainment at school, to collect information from his parents about his daily functioning and ask them to complete the ABAS-3. The BPVS: 3 was used as a screen for general ability and it indicated single word receptive vocabulary in the low average range, and so WISC-V was attempted with Oliver.

The ABAS-3 identified his communication and community use to be significant strengths in which he was functioning in or close to the normal range for his age. However, overall, his adaptive functioning was in the extremely low range with a General Adaptive Composite score of 60 (95% confidence interval 57-63), which placed his abilities at the 0.4th centile. The WISC-V indicated that Oliver had an uneven cognitive profile: his Verbal Comprehension Index score (75) was in the Very Low range while his all his other index scores were in the Extremely Low range, with some scores at the test's floor. His Full Scale IQ score needed to be interpreted cautiously owing to the unusually large spread of scores, but it was in the in the range identified as Moderate Intellectual Disability by the ICD-10 and at a level that would be described as being in the severe learning difficulties range in educational terminology. This was interpreted as verbal communication being a relative strength but that his abilities in this area masked significant difficulties with broader understanding and intellectual abilities. This was likely leading to people overestimating his abilities and so having unrealistic expectations of his ability to manage himself, which contributed to his frustration and which was being expressed in physical and verbal aggression when he could not have what he wanted. It was concluded that, while he might benefit from some basic emotional literacy work and relaxation skills, the majority of the intervention needed to focus on helping those around him to understand his strengths and weaknesses, and supporting them to manage his environment for him.

References

Bayley N (2005) *Bayley Scales of Infant & Toddler Development – Third Edition*. San Antonio, TX: Harcourt Assessment Inc.

Carr A (2006) *The Handbook of Child and Adolescent Clinical Psychology: A contextual approach*. Hove: Routledge.

Elliot C & Smith P (2011) *British Ability Scales: Third Edition*. GL Assessment: Swindon.

Flynn JR (1987) Massive IQ gains in 14 nations: What IQ tests really measure. *Psychological Bulletin* **101** 171–191.

Gore NJ, McGill P, Toogood S, Allen D, Carl Hughes J, Baker P, Hastings RP, Noone SJ & Denne LD (2013) Definition and scope for positive behavioural support. *International Journal of Positive Behavioural Support* **3** (2) 14–23.

Green E, Stroud L, Bloomfield S, Cronje J, Foxcroft C, Hurter K *et al* (2016) *Griffiths Scales of Child Development, Third Edition*. Hogrefe: Oxford

Harrison PL & Oakland T (2015) *Adaptive Behaviour Assessment System-Third Edition*. Torrance, CA: Western Psychological Services.

Jahoda A (2016) Cognitive behavioural therapy. In: N Beail (Ed) *Psychological Therapies and People Who Have Intellectual Disabilities*. Leicester: British Psychological Society

Kaufman A & Kaufman N (2018) *Kaufman Assessment Battery for Children – Second Edition Normative Update*. Circle Pines, MN: American Guidance Service.

McCall RB (1977) Childhood IQ's as predictors of adult educational and occupational status. *Science* **197** (4302) 482–483.

Mullen EM (1995) *Mullen Scales of Early Learning*. San Antonio, TC: Harcourt Assessment Inc.

Nader AM, Courchene V, Dawson M & Souliere I (2016) Does WISC-IV underestimate the intelligence of autistic children? *Journal of Autism Developmental Disorders* **46** (5) 1582–9.

Roid GH, Miller LJ, Pomplun M & Koch C (2013) *Leiter International Performance Scale, Third Edition*. Wood Dale, IL: Stoelting.

Sparrow S, Cicchetti DV & Saulnier CA (2016) *Vineland Adaptive Behaviour Scales-3*. Bloomington, MN. NCS Pearson.

Wechsler D (2010) *Wechsler Adult Intelligence Scale – Fourth UK Edition (WAIS-IV UK)*. San Antonio, TX: Psychological Corporation.

Wechsler D (2013) *Wechsler Preschool & Primary Scale of Intelligence Fourth UK Edition (WPPSI-IV UK)*. San Antonio, TX: Psychological Corporation.

Wechsler D (2016) *Wechsler Intelligence Scale for Children – Fifth UK Edition (WISC-V UK)*. San Antonio, TX: Psychological Corporation.

Chapter 6: Functional assessment

Natasa Momcilovic

Chapter summary

Challenging behaviours are relatively common in children and young people with intellectual disabilities, and they present a major barrier to their achieving good quality of life and having the same opportunities that are accessible to others. Functional assessment is a systematic way of collating and analysing information about problem behaviours that challenge families, carers and organisations, so that appropriate behaviour plans can be developed to minimise the possibility of challenging behaviours occurring in the first place, and, when they do occur, managing them most efficiently. This chapter provides an overview of the functional assessment procedure used with young people with intellectual disability and highlights different methods for data collection and analysis. Helpful suggestions are given for each section explaining the type of information that is sought and how this information informs the development of behaviour support plans. The aim is to enable the reader to develop an understanding of the functional assessment process and guide them towards including functional assessment into their clinical practice.

Introduction

Behavioural disorders in children and young people with intellectual disabilities are relatively common and indeed present a major difficulty not only for families and education professionals, but also for the young people themselves. Behaviour that challenges, more commonly referred to as 'challenging behaviour', is not a psychiatric diagnosis but a summary term used to indicate the presence of a challenge to services, family members and carers.

Individuals with intellectual disabilities are said to be three to five times more likely than the average population to exhibit challenging behaviours (Poppes *et al*, 2010). Challenging behaviour is likely to persist over time in these individuals and the more severe or profound the disabilities they have, the higher the likelihood of challenging behaviour being present (Cormack *et al*, 2000; McIntyre *et al*, 2002; Totsika *et al*, 2008). Some studies document that between 5% and 20% of individuals with intellectual disabilities display challenging behaviours (Ball *et al*, 2004; Emerson, 2001; Lowe *et al*, 1998), whereas other studies note higher rates (Allen, 2000; Cooper *et al*, 2009). A review of studies on aggressive behaviour reported that over 50% of people with intellectual disabilities display some form of aggression (Benson & Brooks, 2008). Rates of severe challenging behaviour have been reported to be 15% in the general population of people with ID (Felce *et al*, 2009), but higher in teenagers and people in their early 20s, and in particular settings, for example 30–40% in hospital settings (NICE, 2015).

The impact of behaviour that challenges may be seen in many ways, including physical injury to the young person or his/her carers, being unable to attend school/college, lack of opportunity to access activities in the community, being unable to make friends, and, later on, the inability to obtain and maintain employment and live independently. It usually causes high levels of stress to parents and carers, and often restricts employment opportunities for parents. There is frequently a significant impact on the wider family, particularly siblings, as they may be the victims of aggression, but also because of the impact on their home environment, including decreased attention from parents, lack of opportunity for family activities and concerns about bringing friends home (Research Autism, 2017). It also compounds social isolation and stigma which is prevalent within this group. Assessment of challenging behaviours is therefore considered an important part of an overall psychiatric assessment with the ultimate goal being achieving a better quality of life.

Definition of challenging behaviours

The term 'challenging behaviour' was introduced to move away from the notion that the problem was located within the person, and instead describes the behaviour as challenging to services ('This person's behaviour presents us with a challenge in how to support him/her' as opposed to, 'this person is being very difficult'). The emphasis was to encourage carers and professionals to find effective ways of understanding a person's behaviour and its underlying causes[1].

Two of the most widely used definitions of 'challenging behaviour' are:

'Culturally abnormal behaviour(s) of such an intensity, frequency or duration that the physical safety of the person or others is likely to be placed in serious jeopardy, or behaviour which is likely to seriously limit use of, or result in the person being denied access to, ordinary community facilities.' (Emerson, 1995)

'Behaviour can be described as challenging when it is of such an intensity, frequency, or duration as to threaten the quality of life and / or the physical safety of the

---

1   For more information, see www.challengingbehaviour.org.uk/

individual or others and it is likely to lead to responses that are restrictive, aversive or result in exclusion.' (Royal College of Psychiatrists, British Psychological Society, Royal College of Speech and Language Therapists, 2007)

The term 'challenging behaviour' incorporates a range of behaviours including verbal and physical aggression, inappropriate social or sexual conduct, self-injury, destructiveness, antisocial and disruptive behaviours, and stereotypical and repetitive behaviours (Benson & Brooks, 2008).

Functional assessment

In line with the current thinking that challenging behaviour is not due to someone being 'very difficult', functional assessment (sometimes referred to as a functional analysis) aims to shed light on the particular needs which a person fulfils through their behaviour which challenges others. It is used to help us identify causes of challenging behaviours, or at least some hypothesis about the reasons for the behaviours displayed, so that an individually tailored behaviour support plan could be developed. A distinction needs to be made between the terms 'Functional Assessment' and 'Functional Analysis', with the former being used to describe the whole process of behaviour assessment while the latter refers to one specific part of that assessment process where we manipulate variables, i.e. what happens before the behaviour and what happens after the behaviour (O'Neill *et al*, 1996).

A change in someone's behaviour that becomes challenging for the carers to deal with is usually the trigger for a referral to Child and Adolescent Mental Health Services (CAMHS). Before their referral, there is often a period during which the behaviour may deteriorate and different management approaches have been tried, with sometimes small and short-lived improvements. The main reason for this is that the challenging behaviours have not been sufficiently and systematically analysed and often the reasons for challenging behaviours have been presumed on the basis of circumstantial evidence.

Functional assessment, in conjunction with overall psychiatric assessment, identifies possible reasons for changes in the behavioural presentation of a young person and this may include a number of factors. For example, physical health problems should be considered in the first instance, as children and young people with intellectual disabilities could be equally affected by physical illness as neurotypical ones, but they may lack the ability to communicate this, or they may lack an understanding of what is happening to them. We also know that young people with intellectual disabilities are more likely to develop mental health disorders such as epilepsy during later childhood or in their teenage years, or depression and psychosis, and these need to be excluded. There are many other significant life events that can affect behavioural change, such as changes of school, changes in the family life, trauma and abuse.

Indirect approaches

A functional assessment is typically carried out by a psychologist or a behaviour specialist in collaboration with parents or primary carers through the use of combined indirect and direct approaches. The indirect approach is where the assessment is based on the results of questionnaires, interviews, rating scales, or daily recording charts that have been completed by parents or primary carers (Addison, 2008).

A first step to identifying the types and extent of problem behaviours is usually to administer questionnaires such as Aberrant Behavior Checklist (ABC), Vineland Adaptive Behavior Scale, Strengths and Difficulties Questionnaire (SDQ), and scales that help understand the function of behaviours such as the Motivational Assessment Scale (MAS), Questions about Behaviour Function (QABF) or Functional Analysis Screening Tool (FAST).

Functional Assessment Interview

The next step is to complete a Functional Assessment Interview (FAI) with the young person's primary carers, i.e. their parents, carers, teachers or respite care providers. The decision as to who will conduct the interview should be based on where the problem behaviours occur, so it may be sufficient to interview just one carer or it may be necessary to interview several relevant carers. Interviewing young people themselves is important, unless this is not possible due to their low cognitive level of functioning or communication difficulties.

A Functional Assessment Interview is a semi-structured interview that is divided into 11 major sections and it begins with the description of problem behaviours (see Functional Assessment Interview Form, Appendix 1 on page 86).

Description of problem behaviour

It is important to understand when the behaviour first became a problem and the type of onset, i.e. gradual or sudden. Gradual onset possibly indicates a long-term problem behaviour that has over time become more difficult to manage due to a range of factors, such as the young person becoming bigger and stronger, their behaviour being inadvertently reinforced by others, or an increase in the extent of self-injury or injury to others. Sudden onset usually indicates the presence of an event that has somehow impacted their behaviour and may include a health problem in a young person, a change of medication, a change in their environment or a change in how they are managed.

We start with labelling the behaviour (e.g. pinching) describing physical movements that are performed, how long the behaviour lasts once it starts, how frequently the behaviour occurs in a typical day/week, and the intensity of behaviour, and this helps us to understand the impact on the young person and their carers. One problematic behaviour rarely occurs in isolation from other behaviours, which is a more common presentation, and therefore understanding co-variance and sequence is important. For example, pinching may occur before spitting and throwing objects. This is relevant for the development of a behaviour support plan, as behaviours that occur together often have the same function and we may be able to intervene at the start of the first behaviour in the sequence to prevent escalation.

Setting events

The next focus is on ecological events that do not necessarily happen immediately before or after the problem behaviour, but will still affect whether these behaviours occur. We need to establish whether a young person is taking medications, including prescription or alternative medications and supplements given by parents, whether there has been change in the medication used and how it impacted the behaviour of the young person, and if there are any known side effects. We need to enquire about the presence of medical or physical problems, which may be causing pain and discomfort, and which may happen periodically, such as period pain or hay fever, or be constant, such as arthritis. The next area is to look at the person's typical sleep pattern in order to establish any recent changes, such as a lack of sleep that may be impacting on the day time behaviours, which many studies have found to be related (Wiggs & Stores, 1996).

The next step is finding details about the young person's diet and eating routines, including how often they eat, times of meals, calorie intake and any restrictions in their diet, which could be due to personal preference or imposed by carers for health/religious reasons. For example, an escalation of problem behaviours around reduced access to food and before mealtimes is common in young people with Prader-Willi syndrome, which is characterised with constant craving for food, constant hunger and food-seeking behaviours, such as hoarding food or eating frozen food.

We next look at the typical daily schedule of activities for a young person in order to determine whether they are usually associated with problems. Here we are interested in how the person can predict their typical routines and whether they have any opportunity to make choices about what is going to happen. Being able to have some control over situations is known to reduce problem behaviours in young people.

Finally, we consider the number of people in home and school and the impact this has on a young person. For example, a young person who prefers isolation and quiet environments may find a busy classroom particularly difficult to tolerate and may resort to problem behaviours to escape that environment.

Specific events/situations

In this section we focus our enquires on specific situations in which problem behaviours occur and do not occur, including when and where they happen, who is with a young person at that time and whether it is related to specific activities. By learning about those specific circumstances, and about combinations of several aspects being present at the same time, we can help predict when problem behaviours could occur and therefore develop behaviour support plans to minimise those situations and prevent the need for the young person to engage in problem behaviours in the first place.

It is also important to identify the functions that the problem behaviours serve, keeping in mind that behaviours may be used to either obtain something that is desirable, which is referred to as 'positive reinforcement', or avoid something that is undesirable, which is referred to as 'negative reinforcement'. For both of the types of reinforcement, the behaviours could be driven by socially mediated events, including obtaining and avoiding attention and activities, and by obtaining and avoiding internal events such as obtaining sensory stimulation or avoiding pain. The table below shows this categorisation (O'Neill *et al*, 1996).

Table 6.1: Consequences maintaining problem behaviour

Obtain internal stimulation	Obtain attention	Obtain activities or objects	Escape/avoid internal stimulation	Escape/avoid attention	Escape/avoid tasks activities
Visual stimulation Endorphin release	Smiles Hugs Frowns	Food Toys Money Trip to a shop	Sinus pain Period pain Itching Hunger Thirst	Smiles Hugs Frowns Hugs Corrections	Hard tasks Change in routine Unpredictability
Positive *Automatic* *Reinforcement*	*Positive* *Reinforcement* *Social*	*Positive* *Reinforcement* *Tangible/activity*	*Negative* *Automatic* *Reinforcement*	*Negative Reinforcement* *Escape motivated social*	*Negative Reinforcement* *Escape motivated task*

Our next consideration is to determine the efficiency of the problem behaviour in obtaining desirable or avoiding non-desirable events through understanding how much physical effort is required, and how quickly and consistently they achieve the desired aim. Behaviours that are quicker in helping someone achieve what they want, and more consistent in achieving this, tend to be more frequently used. For example, a non-verbal child may resort to screaming while standing next to a refrigerator rather than using PECS (Picture Exchange Communication System) symbols to indicate what they want as their parent is more likely to arrive faster and start offering favourite food items from the refrigerator. We therefore need to establish whether a young person has alternative functional behaviours that they already know how to perform and that could bring them the same desired outcome, as we may need to encourage them to use it more through positive reinforcement.

Understanding someone's communication style, both in terms of their receptive and expressive ability, is important for building a behaviour support plan. Any support plan should include information about their use and understanding of language, use and understanding of gesture, and use of alternative communication systems such as Makaton or PECS. Equally important is finding out the best ways to help the young person learn new things and their personal preferences, including items, activities or types of praise which can be used for positive reinforcement once we start designing our behaviour support plan.

Information about previous and current management strategies and behavioural interventions is also relevant, as considering new ways of intervening with problem behaviours is, contrary to popular belief, not about discovering some new management approaches, often referred to as a 'magic wand', but in adjustments of current strategies.

By analysing this obtained information, we can start developing a hypothesis about when problem behaviours happen and how they are maintained, and the next step is confirming our hypothesis through direct approaches to functional assessment.

Direct approaches

In contrast to the indirect approach, the direct approach involves the direct and natural observation of the behaviour by the person who is conducting the assessment, as it occurs in the natural setting. Observing the child in their natural environment at home and at school, or sometimes respite and in the community, gives us an opportunity to consider our hypothesis about the cause and the maintenance of problem behaviour. These are best conducted as 'fly on the wall', non-intrusive observations by a professional with whom the child is unfamiliar as this will avoid any changes in their usual behaviour in that setting which can happen once a young person is aware that they are being observed. Although natural observations are best completed across as many settings and over as much time per day as possible, for practical reasons we tend to plan our observations during the times that we know may be problematic, such as during transitions, during tasks when demands are put on a young person or during unstructured time when less adult support is provided, such as play time. These observations are also referred to as Structured Descriptive Assessments (e.g. Anderson & Long, 2002).

Other information obtained through anecdotal or written descriptions, incident reports, frequency counts, interval recording systems, antecedent-behaviour-consequence (ABC) charts (see Appendix 1 on page 86) and videotaping should also be analysed. We hope that through analysing these recordings we are able to establish the link between the behaviour that occurs, antecedent events that set up conditions for the behaviour occurring, and consequent events that maintain the behaviour, which will lead us to a better understanding of its particular function for a young person.

While we complete our observations, we may also consider using Functional Analysis manipulations, which are used for testing hypotheses regarding variables or events most strongly related to the occurrence of problem behaviours. Therefore, we can manipulate structural or antecedent events to test a hypothesis about which events or variables might cause the onset of behaviours, or we can manipulate the consequences of the problem behaviours by arranging different situations and specific consequences which are provided contingent upon the occurrence of specific problem behaviours. Functional analysis manipulations are predominantly used in research for many reasons, some of which include difficulties in controlling factors that may influence our observation, and ethical issues, such as those encountered when observing significant aggressive and self-injurious behaviours.

Recording behaviour

Problem behaviour is recorded through observations completed in real time by noting the frequency and duration of the behaviours as they occur. There are three main time sampling methods that could be considered here, including partial interval time sampling (record the behaviour if it occurs at any point in a given time period), whole interval (record the behaviour if it occurs throughout a given time period) and momentary sampling (record the behaviour if it occurs at the point of observation only, e.g. every five seconds). The professional completing the observation would be the one to guide this process and decide on the use of one particular sampling method, depending on the type of baseline data one is trying to capture. The practicality of using these recording methods should also be considered, as parents/carers or class teachers often need to complete these observations.

The first step in observing problem behaviour is to give it an operational description, describing exactly what type of behaviour should be observed. Descriptions should explain succinctly what type of behaviour it is, how it is performed and when it starts and ends, as failing to do this may lead to different types of behaviour being observed. Behaviour recording is typically conducted over a two-week period although this will be influenced by the frequency of the problem behaviour; for example, for more frequent behaviours one week should be sufficient.

Once behaviour recording is completed, the professional sets about analysing the recordings and interpreting descriptive data, which leads to identifying specific patterns and confirming or disputing hypothetical functions that have been formulated previously. An important and very practical point needs to be made here: if our hypothesis about the causes and maintenance of problem behaviours has been confirmed through simply recording the data on ABC charts, and we have implemented behaviour management strategies that have reduced the occurrence of problem behaviours, there is no need to go through the whole procedure described above as our hypothesis has been proven and a successful behaviour support plan implemented.

Behaviour support plans

Behaviour support plans result from the functional assessment process and clearly define what will be done to reduce problem behaviour. The aim is to improve the consistency across settings and among all the young person's carers. However, it is important to recognise that challenging behaviour can occur for very complex reasons and there will be individuals for whom those reasons remain unclear, even after a functional assessment has been carried out. Regardless, plans that have been made should help with maintaining the consistency of approach and offer further opportunities for continued assessment.

Behaviour support plans should consist of reactive and proactive strategies for the management of challenging behaviours.

Reactive plan

Reactive plans are how one should behave in the event of challenging behaviour occurring by providing step-by-step advice on how to minimise the likelihood that the challenging behaviour will escalate. A reactive plan should be informed by a functional assessment and guided by the principal of implementing the least intrusive and least restrictive intervention first, for example distracting someone with a preferred object or activity, as opposed to responding to their behaviour directly by telling them to stop doing what they are doing. More restrictive interventions, such as physical restraint or medication used to calm a person down, should only be considered as a last resort, and only when non-physical interventions have been exhausted, following a multi-disciplinary consultation with the family (Addison, 2008). Reactive plans might include non-physical responses such as planned ignoring, giving reminders, distraction, giving the person what they want or withdrawing from a situation.

Proactive plan

A proactive plan describes what you are doing on a day-to-day basis to help minimise the likelihood that someone will resort to challenging behaviour in the first place. The proactive plan looks at all aspects of the person's life by considering ideas from multiple sources with the aim of enhancing a person's quality of life and making the reactive plan redundant in the long term. Again, management strategies used here should be directly informed by the functional assessment and used consistently across all settings. Proactive strategies may include removing triggers for challenging behaviour, teaching replacement skills, changing the young person's environment, adapting interaction styles to their preferences, providing motivating rewards, providing a consistent routine and structure to their days and communicating this efficiently to them, providing boundaries and additional support adequate for their individual needs.

Case vignette

Child A was a 12-year-old girl with moderate intellectual disability and autistic spectrum disorder. She had a history of challenging behaviours, which were impacting on her school and home life. The main challenge for her carers was her obsession with alarm bells, fire alarms, sirens on emergency vehicles, school bells, car alarms and loudspeaker announcements in shops. She talked about them at all times and would cover her ears and laugh if she heard them from a distance, but she would panic if they were close by and run away, which was putting her personal safety at risk. An additional difficulty at home was her obsession with being first at everything, which was having an impact on all the family as her favourite leisure activity of playing board games with her family always ended in her becoming angry and engaging in aggressive behaviour.

Functional assessment was completed including interviews with her family and educational staff, and behavioural observations were completed at school. The observation confirmed that she was talking about alarms every few minutes, which was disruptive for her academic work and she routinely declined to engage in activities in fear that an alarm might go off.

A behaviour support plan was developed as part of which it was agreed with her school that the family would be provided with a schedule of planned alarm tests, so that she could be prepared in time, ear defenders could be provided, and she would be offered individual support from the teaching staff. In conjunction, she was provided with Graded Exposure work for her alarm phobia, which was conducted in the clinic and in her local community. A fire station was approached to provide an opportunity for siren exposure while she used relaxation strategies advised by the clinical staff. In addition, her mother took her on frequent trips to a local store to buy her favourite items, where she was exposed for increasingly longer times to different bells, tills and loudspeakers within the store. This approach resulted in a reduction in her anxiety levels and over period of several months she became able to participate in several leisure activities in her community.

A behaviour modification approach was used to address her obsessions with being the winner when playing boarding games. A programme was designed where family members deliberately kept their playing cards in several smaller piles, as her observation of their card stack becoming bigger was the trigger for her anger. A reward system was introduced where the winner would receive a social reward of clapping and cheering by others, and all the losers would receive a booby prize of a sweet. As the young person was more interested in having the sweet, she started wanting to lose in the game to receive it. The sweets were initially offered every time she lost a game, and then they were gradually phased out, initially by not actively offering them to her and then moving them off the table. This approach resulted in reduction in her aggressive behaviour and restoration of her enjoyment during play on board games.

A Behaviour Support Plan should be a 'working' document that is continuously updated to reflect any increased knowledge or understanding of the person and how best to support them. An increased understanding may enable us to make changes in the person's life that will result in a reduction in their challenging behaviour or support us to help them find alternatives to using their challenging behaviour.

A more detailed description of management approaches used for challenging behaviours and creating behaviour support plans can be found in practical handbooks specifically aimed at this topic (McBrien & Felce,1992; Hardy & Joyce, 2011).

Additional information on functional assessment, behaviour management plans and resources can be found on the following websites:

The Challenging Behaviour Foundation (www.challengingbehaviour.org.uk)

Mencap (www.mencap.org.uk)

The British Institute of Intellectual disabilities (www.bild.org.uk)

NICE Overview: Challenging behaviour and intellectual disabilities: prevention and interventions for people with intellectual disabilities whose behaviour challenges (www.nice.org.uk/guidance/ng11)

How to deal with challenging behaviour in children – NHS (https://www.nhs.uk/conditions/social-care-and-support-guide/caring-for-children-and-young-people/how-to-deal-with-challenging-behaviour-in-children/)

Managing Challenging Behaviour Factsheet - Cerebra (https://cerebra.org.uk/download/factsheet-managing-challenging-behaviour)

A functional Assessment Interview Form can be found at:

www.marshall.edu/atc/files/2013/07/Functional-Assessment-Interview-FAI-93-103.pdf

Conclusion

Functional assessment is vital for effective behaviour support and leads to improvements in quality of life for young people with intellectual disabilities as well as their families. Challenging behaviours range from mildly disruptive to highly complex, and they inevitably have a negative impact on a young person's relationships with others, as well as minimising choices that are available to them. The clinician's aim is to enable the families, schools and other agencies, such as respite care, to develop their understanding of the individual needs of a young person that presents with challenging behaviours and consider most helpful ways of supporting them in their natural environments. The functional assessments process highlights the need for collaborative approach between clinicians, carers and agencies, and encourages ongoing information gathering that will support successful development of behaviour support plan. Clinicians have a key role in leading this process through their theoretical knowledge of behaviour therapy and practical experience in the application of behavioural and cognitive behavioural interventions.

References

Addison M (2008) Using a functional assessment to understand challenging behaviour and identify ways of supporting behaviour change; Information Sheet, Challenging Behaviour – Supporting Change; Challenging Behaviour Foundation website (https://www.challengingbehaviour.org.uk/learning-disability-files/10_Challenging_Behaviour_Supporting_Change_2008.pdf)

Allen D (2000) Recent research on physical aggression in persons with intellectual disability: an overview. *Journal of Intellectual and Developmental Disability* **25** (1) 41– 57.

Anderson C & Long E (2002) Use of a structured descriptive assessment methodology to identify variables affecting problem behavior. *Journal of applied behavior analysis* **35** (2) 137–154.

Ball T, Bush A & Emerson E (2004) Psychological interventions for severely challenging behaviours shown by people with intellectual disabilities. *Aims & Scope* **38**.

Benson BA & Brooks WT (2008) Aggressive challenging behaviour and intellectual disability. *Current Opinion in Psychiatry* **21** (5) 454–458.

Cooper SA, Smiley E, Jackson A, Finlayson J, Allan L, Mantry D & Morrison J (2009) Adults with intellectual disabilities: prevalence, incidence and remission of aggressive behaviour and related factors. *Journal of Intellectual Disability Research* **53** (3) 217– 232.

Cormack KFM, Brown AC & Hastings RP (2000) Behavioural and emotional difficulties in students attending schools for children and adolescents with severe intellectual disability. *Journal of Intellectual Disability Research* **44** (2) 124–129.

Emerson E (2001) *Challenging Behaviour: Analysis and intervention in people with severe intellectual disabilities.* Cambridge University Press.

Emerson E (1995) cited in Emerson E (2001, 2nd edition) *Challenging Behaviour: Analysis and intervention in people with intellectual disabilities.* Cambridge University Press.

Felce D, Kerr M & Hastings RP (2009) A general practice-based study of the relationship between indicators of mental illness and challenging behaviour among adults with intellectual disabilities. *Journal of Intellectual Disability Research* **53** (3) 243–254.

Hardy S & Joyce T (2011) Challenging Behaviour: Practical Resource Addressing Ways of Providing Positive Behavioural Support to People with Intellectual disabilities Whose Behaviour is Described as Challenging. New ed. Edition. Hove: Pavilion Publishing & Media Ltd.

Lowe K, Felce D, Perry J, Baxter H & Jones E (1998) The characteristics and residential situations of people with severe intellectual disability and the most severe challenging behaviour in Wales. *Journal of Intellectual Disability Research* **42** (5) 375–389.

McBrien J & Felce D (1992) *Working with People who have Severe Learning Disability and Challenging Behaviour: A practical handbook on the behavioural approach*. BILD Publications.

McIntyre LL, Blacher J & Baker BL (2002) Behaviour/mental health problems in young adults with intellectual disability: the impact on families. *Journal of Intellectual Disability Research* **46** (3) 239–249.

NICE Guideline (2015) *Challenging behaviour and intellectual disabilities: prevention and interventions for people with intellectual disabilities whose behaviour challenges* [online]. Available at: https://www.nice.org.uk/guidance/ng11 (accessed June 2020).

O'Neill RE, Horner RH, Albin RW, Storey K & Sprague JR (1996) *Functional Assessment and Program Development for Problem Behaviour: A practical handbook, 2nd Revised edition*. Wadsworth Publishing Co Inc.

Poppes et al (2010) Frequency and severity of challenging behavior in people with profound intellectual and multiple disabilities. *Research in developmental disabilities* **31** (6) 1269–75.

Research Autism (2017) Challenging behaviour and Autism. http://www.researchautism.net/issues/52/challenging-behaviour-and-autism

Royal College of Psychiatrists, British Psychological Society, Royal College of Speech and Language Therapists (2007) *Challenging behaviour – a unified approach*.

Totsika V, Toogood S, Hastings RP & Lewis S (2008) Persistence of challenging behaviours in adults with intellectual disability over a period of 11 years. *Journal of Intellectual Disability Research* **52** (5) 446–457.

Wiggs L & Stores G (1996) Sleep problems in children with severe intellectual disabilities: what help is being provided? *Journal of Applied Research in Intellectual Disabilities* **9** 159–164.

Resources

Aman MG, Singh NN, Stewart AW & Field CJ (1985) The aberrant behavior checklist: a behavior rating scale for the assessment of treatment effects. *American Journal of Mental Deficiency.* 89 (5) 485–91.

Sparrow SS, Cicchetti DV & Balla DA (2005) *Vineland-II Adaptive Behavior Scales: Survey Forms Manual*. Circle Pines, MN: AGS Publishing.

Goodman R (1997) The Strengths and Difficulties Questionnaire: A research note. *Journal of Child Psychology and Psychiatry* **38** 581–586.

Durand VM & Crimmins DB (1992) *The Motivation Assessment Scale (MAS) administration guide*. Topeka, KS: Monaco and Associates.

Paclawskyj TR (1998) *Questions About Behavioral Function (QABF): A behavioral checklist for Functional Assessment of aberrant behavior.*

Iwata BA & DeLeon IG (1995) The Functional Analysis Screening Tool (FAST). University of Florida, FL.

Appendix 1

ABC Record Chart

Name:

Day, Date and Time of Incident:

Definition of Behaviour:

Antecedent events

In this row, with the following questions in mind, provide a step-by-step description of exactly what you observed prior to the behaviour, or at the same time as the behaviour occurred.

1. Where was the person and exactly what were they doing?
2. Was anyone else around or had anyone just left?
3. Had a request been made of the person?
4. Had the person asked for, or did they want, something to eat or drink?
5. Had the person asked for, or did they want, a specific object or activity?
6. Had an activity just ended or been cancelled?
7. Where were you and what were you doing?
8. How did the person's mood appear, e.g. happy, sad, angry, withdrawn or distressed?
9. Did the person seem to be communicating anything through their behaviour, e.g. I don't want…;I want…?

Behaviour

In this row, provide a step-by-step description of exactly what the person did, e.g. he ran out of the living room, stood in the kitchen doorway and punched his head with his right hand for approximately 1 minute.

Consequent events

In this row, with the following questions in mind, provide a step-by-step description of the exact events that occurred immediately after the behaviour.

1. Exactly how did you respond to the behaviour? Give a step-by-step description.
2. How did the person respond to your reaction to the behaviour?
3. Was there anyone else around who responded to, or showed a reaction to, the behaviour?
4. Did the person's behaviour result in them gaining anything they did not have before the behaviour was exhibited, e.g. attention from somebody (positive or negative); an object, food or drink; or escape from an activity or situation?

Signature:

Chapter 7: Communication

Karen Lewis and Stephanie Carr

Chapter summary

This chapter explores communication when working with young people with intellectual disabilities and supports and adjustments that can be made to enable them to reach their communicative potential. Discussion will include sections on autism spectrum conditions, moderate intellectual disability, severe intellectual disability, profound and multiple intellectual disability, developmental language disorder, augmentative and alternative communication, including sign and the Picture Exchange Communication System, environmental adjustments and advice on supporting a young person's communication on an everyday basis.

Introduction

Communication is considered to be the act of transferring the thoughts and feelings of one person to another. It can occur via several methods, most frequently speech, then gesture and body 'language'. Especially important when considering people with intellectual disabilities (ID) is that communication can be both intentional and unintentional.

The Intellectual disability Census (2017) highlights that 70% of people with ID have additional communication needs. As the severity of ID increases, communication impairment also increases; those with the most severe intellectual disabilities will also have the most severe communication impairments. As such, they will need the most adjustment to support them to make their needs known.

Communication refers to several simultaneous complex cognitive and physical processes that are developmental in nature. It is most commonly split into three components: Receptive Language, Expressive Language and Speech. A person with ID may have a more significant impairment in one area, or have equal needs in each.

Receptive Language is the ability to take in, understand and process information. It depends on an individual's ability to listen, process and know what words mean. As the skills become more advanced, it also includes the ability to understand concepts and grammatical aspects of language.

Expressive Language is a person's ability to convey their thoughts, feelings or needs through whatever means is effective for them. For a neurotypical person, this typically involves selecting the precise words and sentence construction to most effectively externalise a thought, feeling or need.

In addition to the above, executive and social language skills are interwoven; a person may be able to understand the individual words in a sentence but, when combined into a metaphor or with an abstract concept, the person's ability to understand the meaning or inferred intent can decrease. Speech refers to the sounds that are produced by a person which combine to form recognisable words. There are 24 individual consonant sounds and 20 vowel sounds used within British English.

When considering communication and ID, we understand that communication is proportionally impaired, for example someone with a more severe intellectual disability will have more difficulties communicating than a typical young person with a mild or moderate intellectual disability. Some additional areas for consideration are explored below.

Profound and multiple learning disabilities (PMLD)

People with PMLD are generally thought to be young people who have cognitive skills at or around a Full Scale Intelligence Quotient (FSIQ) of 20. Due to this level of cognitive difficulty, young people will be able to understand the most frequently used language and routines around them, understanding usually up to 50 words, and require a great deal of adaptation/consideration from the people around them to understand their feelings and needs, which is often achieved through observation. They may not develop intentional communication and can be considered to be at a pre-verbal communication stage, i.e. their skills are at a stage where they are unable to access verbal communication. A person's level of comfort and occupation should always be considered using a tool such as the Disability Distress Assessment Tool (DISTAT) to understand distress and pain presentations for young people, as addressing this need can significantly improve a person's quality of life and reduce behavioural need.

Autism spectrum conditions (ASC)

Children with autism and intellectual disabilities will have additional communication needs to those without a diagnosis of autism but with a similar IQ. This can be explained in part by difficulties with motivation/sharing another's agenda, joint attention and specific needs with executive language and social functions, such as inferencing, reciprocity and abstract language. Several specific interventions can be used to support young people with autism, which are discussed below.

Pre-verbal, non-verbal and selective mutism

Some people with intellectual disabilities do not, or cannot, use speech to communicate. These young people usually fall into three groups:

- **Pre-verbal.** These young people are not able to use words to communicate due to their developmental level. They are typically at a developmental stage prior to nine months. They may or may not use babble, however they will not be at an intentional communication stage.

- **Non-verbal.** Young people described as non-verbal will typically understand words and may have contextually well-developed skills understanding language, however they will not use speech to communicate. The reasons for this are not always clear, however variously speech disorder, communicative intent (particularly in autism) and specific neurological conditions such as agenesis of the corpus collosum can be relevant.

- **Selective mutism.** Some young people who can speak become unable to in specific or more general situations. This is attributed to anxiety and usually called selective mutism. Communication assessment is required for these young people in order to rule out communication disorders or acquired conditions, however treatment is usually anxiety based.

Developmental language disorder (DLD)

Children with intellectual disabilities may have communication difficulties 'over and above' their cognitive needs, and the communication profile may not be indicative of autism or another condition associated with language impairment. In this case, DLD can be considered, it can impact on any area of communication development and for those young people where the impairment is significant. Although there is no definitive intervention, behavioural language learning interventions have proven effective.

Speech disorders

There are a number of different reasons why a young person's speech may sound different from his or her peers. Some of these can be due to generalised delays which can be common for young people whose overall development is at an earlier level. However, at times, normal delays can pervade over time and in other cases a young person's speech may be disordered (sound different due to unusual processes). This can be due to several reasons and requires the assessment and treatment by a Speech and Language Therapist (SLT). Speech disorders can impact severely on a person's quality of life, limiting his or her ability to communicate to an extreme degree. A young person with a intellectual disability and speech disorder may require an additional communication system to support their day-to-day communication.

Speech and language therapy role

As communication specialists, Speech and Language Therapists offer a range of opportunities to the multi-disciplinary team and input for a young person:

- Assessment and review.
- Multidisciplinary differential diagnosis.
- Therapy/Management/Programmes.
- Advice and recommendations.
- Consultation.
- Training.

Assessment

Understanding a person's use and understanding of language can be key to understanding their needs and treatment opportunities, for example a young person who does not have established emotional concept understanding will not be able to access spoken, psychological therapies such as cognitive or dialectical behaviour therapy. There are many communication models (e.g.*Input-Output; *Means, Reasons and Opportunities). Assessment of underlying speech and language skills alongside consideration of these components form the basis of intervention.

Assessment typically includes a developmental case history plus formal and informal assessments and observations. A range of formal assessments/checklists are used with children and young people (CYP) with ID, but these are generally not standardised for this population so results can give guidance only regarding levels of ability. A 15-year-old CYP with language levels around a three year level will have broader communication skills that have developed over their lifetime.

Materials and procedures may need adaptations specific to the CYP's needs and are therefore non-standard, for example carrying out an assessment over several sessions or involving a third person.

Assessment of a CYP with ID and/or autism spectrum condition (ASC) involves a number of different areas to achieve a differential diagnosis and identify areas of need. Findings are considered within a developmental framework and contribute to developing a communication profile.

Typically, areas assessed may include:

- speech clarity (articulation)
- speech sound development (phonology)
- attention and listening (including hearing)
- visual and perceptual skills (including visual acuity)
- understanding of spoken language (receptive skills)
- memory and processing
- expressive language skills including form (grammar/syntax) and content (semantics)
- social use of language (pragmatics) and social communication skills
- communicative functions
- non-verbal communication skills (facial expression; gesture; intonation; body language; augmentative communication systems)
- environment (partners; physical).

Communication difficulties often occur alongside co-existing conditions such as sensory impairments, ADHD, ASC and mental health diagnoses. Multi-disciplinary team involvement is essential to provide information across all areas and consider how they interact to impact the individual's communication skills.

Models of intervention/approaches

Functional communication training is the blending of behavioural and communication interventions which are used to progressively modify a person's behaviours of concern into a communicative behaviour serving the same need/ function/meaning over several shaping stages. It is reliant on a detailed understanding of that person's use of behaviour (achieved via Functional Analysis), their skills and existing communicative repertoire.

Functional communication skills allow an individual to express needs, wants, feelings and preferences in a way that is understandable to others. Functional communication skills allow a CYP to express themselves, minimise communication breakdown and the need to use of behaviours of concern. It is usually at a basic developmental level, reflecting skills which typically emerge in the first year of life. CYP with developmental delays or significant language impairments may still be working on these skills when much older. Functional communication skills may include idiosyncratic signs, gestures, vocalisations/speech attempts and pictorial supports. Teaching of these skills should be frequent, repeated and in the individual's natural environments within everyday routines and contexts

Modelling is basically 'showing'. Therapists and communication partners demonstrate to the learner the skill they wish them to acquire (e.g. pointing to a picture to make a choice). Individuals with ID need frequent exposure to partners using the skill in order to understand it and then do it. Learning is most effective when modelling happens in relevant and reinforcing real-life situations. Once a skill has been acquired in one situation with one communication partner it can be generalised across multiple contexts with a range of communication partners.

Common specific interventions and support tools

Intensive Interaction is an approach to teaching those at an early stage of communication development. It aims to develop the pre-linguistic communication fundamentals based on interactions between parents and babies. It teaches interactive elements of communication without necessarily using spoken language. It treats all behaviour as communication and is controlled by the CYP. The CYP leads the activity and the partner develops the content and flow by responding to their actions. The partner can imitate/mirror the CYP by joining in what they are doing, using facial expression, tone and body language. The partner must 'tune in' to the CYP and go at their pace, building in pauses to allow them to decide what to do next. No spoken language is introduced unless the CYP does so first.

This encourages:

- building attention and concentration
- building shared attention
- learning sequences
- turn-taking
- eye contact
- using facial expressions
- vocalisations with meaning.

Intensive Interaction should be fun for everyone. It is best done frequently, somewhere without distractions and with a familiar partner.

Social skills training: teaching young people how to become effective social communicators is often a vital part of becoming a successful communicator; if you know the words to use but don't know how to initiate conversation or talk to a new person, your communication interaction is still likely to fail. There are several manualised interventions for teaching social skills for young people with ID, both with and without autism. It is important to note again that social skills are developmental and a knowledge of that young person's pre-existing skills is essential. Understandably, these should be group-based interventions.

Visual structures: Everyone uses visual information within their daily lives. It is important to know an individual's level of symbolic understanding (objects, photographs, pictures/drawings, symbols, gestures and sign language, spoken or written words) in order to provide appropriate supports.

Reasons to use visuals:

■ Permanent.
■ Allow time for language processing.
■ Prepare for transitions.
■ Individual can see what you mean.
■ Individual knows what to expect and is less anxious.
■ Promote independence.
■ Transferable between environments.
■ They don't have an attitude.

Commonly used visual supports for people with ID and/or ASC include:

■ Objects of reference
■ Now… next boards
■ Visual timetables
■ Task breakdowns/sequences
■ Choice boards
■ Communication books
■ Symbols including the Picture Exchange Communication System (PECS)
■ Social Stories
■ Makaton signing
■ Communication Passports.

Some of these are discussed below.

Symbols are used by everyone to convey information efficiently (e.g. toilets, road signs and exit symbols). Young people with any degree of ID can benefit from using symbols to support their understanding of what other people are saying, as well as to express themselves.

There are many symbol sets available and individual symbols are usually paired with the printed word/phrase they represent. The most frequently used symbol sets in the UK are Picture Communication Symbols (PCS), Widgit Symbols, Symbolstix and Blissymbols. Symbolic language systems (e.g. Blissymbols) are much more powerful than pictures (e.g. PCS or Widgit), but will be initially harder to understand and learn. There are also some graphic symbol systems such as Minsymbols™ and Dynasyms™ associated with specific hi-tech communication aids.

Choosing a symbol set requires careful consideration of a number of factors, matched against a potential user's developmental needs and abilities. Consideration needs to be made of an individual's levels of symbolic understanding. There is a hierarchy developmentally: individual's will first understand what meaning objects represent, then photographs, then line drawings, then symbols and finally the written word. Symbols provide added value over objects, photos and individual pictures in their ability to represent concepts that are difficult to convey otherwise (e.g. more, tomorrow) and the ability to combine these to represent phrases/ sentences. Adding symbols to words (e.g. making documents 'accessible') does not mean an individual will automatically understand the information given. A way to begin to add meaning to symbols is to pair them with real objects where possible, and then photographs, but this is only feasible for concrete concepts. Use of symbols can also be modelled and paired with verbal commands, and colour-coding of items can also be a useful teaching tool.

Other considerations when choosing symbols and symbol sets include:

- How pictorial/concrete are they?
- How transparent/guessable are they?
- How flexible are they?
- How consistent are they regarding visual elements/able to be combined?
- How visually complex are they, including use of colour versus black and white?
- Are they consistent across communication environments?
- Do they match the vocabulary/grammatical needs of the individual?

Talking mats are conversation tools for acquiring views and opinions of a wide range of users. It consists of a door/car mat (or similar) and sets of pictures. Originally designed by Murphy and Cameron (1998), University of Stirling, to help people with ID express their choices, views and feelings, talking mats are currently used with anyone struggling to hold a spoken conversation or discuss difficult topics. The structured approach focuses attention, reduces memory and language demands, and helps users gather their thoughts. They avoid direct confrontation and allow participants to convey negative or embarrassing thoughts they are too scared to say aloud.

Talking mats are invaluable tools to encourage interaction and conversation; plan activities; encourage involvement in goal setting; enable involvement in life planning; explore differences of opinions; assist advocacy and explore sensitive issues.

Communication passports provide a practical, person-centred way to share key information about people with complex communication difficulties. A communication passport describes the person's most effective means of communication and gives strategies through which partners can support the individual. Information is gathered from past and present, from many people who know the person, and from different contexts.

A communication passport is a way to support the person with communication difficulties across transitions, collating information (including the person's views where possible) and compiling this into a clear, positive and accessible format. This helps communication partners get to know the person and interact/respond consistently to help the individual reach their communicative potential.

The communication passport belongs to the person, although staff or family may help the person use it appropriately and update it. Passports are especially important for transitions and when new people come into the person's life. *CALL Scotland provides templates for producing communication passports.

Social stories are a social learning tool originally designed by *Caroline Gray to help people with ASC and their communication partners better understand aspects of social communication. A true social story uses 10 defining criteria to guide its development and implementation:

- Meaningful, reassuring sharing of social information; at least 50% of social stories should celebrate achievements.
- Topic is clearly introduced, main body adds detail, and conclusion reinforces and summarises information.
- Answers 'wh' questions.
- Is written in first or third person.

- Uses positive language.
- Contains descriptive sentences, with an option to include any from five other sentence types.
- Describes rather than directs.
- Is tailored to the abilities and interests of individual.
- May use pictures to add meaning to the text.
- The title should meet all applicable social story criteria.

Social stories do not aim to stop behaviours of concern but rather guide the CYP towards alternative, socially valid options and strategies while describing who might help and how.

The **Picture Exchange Communication System (PECS)** was developed in *1984 by Frost and Bondy. It allows CYP with limited means, to communicate using pictures. CYP are taught to initiate by approaching a communication partner and trading a picture of an item in exchange for that item. An individual can use PECS to communicate requests, thoughts, or anything that can be represented pictorially. PECS involves six stages (i.e. How to communicate; Distance and Persistence; Picture Discrimination; Sentence Structure; Answering Questions and Commenting), beginning with the exchange of simple pictures and building to a range of 'sentences' on a strip handed to the communication partner. Originally developed for use with people with ASC, PECS is now used broadly including with people with ID.

Augmentative and Alternative Communication (AAC) is a range of strategies and tools to help people who struggle with using speech as their primary means of expression. AAC can be low-tech, using simple letter or picture boards, or high-tech, using sophisticated computer or tablet-based systems. AAC helps someone to communicate as effectively as possible, in as many situations as possible. When considering AAC, specialist assessment is often required alongside specialist support. Often a young person will have trials of different equipment to ensure the best match.

Sign language and Makaton Sign Language are languages for the hearing impaired and deaf community, however for young people with ID they are often used as an augmentation to both understanding and expression. Sign language represents words with hand and arm movements and often involves expressive use of facial expression.

Although there are several systems in use both nationally and internationally, the sign component of Makaton is usually the most familiar. Makaton supports the use of speech and sign alongside each other to support messages. It can be helpful to add meaning to a sentence or to support a person with unclear speech.

Objects of Reference (OoR) are objects that represent a person, place or activity. They are typically used with young people with the most severe communication impairment. Their use must be systematic, routine based and consistent in order to aid understanding. The object aims to help a young person be informed about what is happening next. They should be highly individualised and highly representative of the thing that they represent. For example:

- A ball from the ball pool to represent the sensory room.
- A swimming band to represent the swimming pool.
- An air freshener the same as the one in the school taxi to say the taxi is coming.

Communication difficulties and mental health

Between 50% and 90% of people with ID have communication difficulties; about 80% of people with severe ID fail to acquire effective speech and around 20% of people with ID have no intentional communication skills.

CYP with difficulties in areas such as attention, memory, processing, vocabulary, grammar, comprehension, emotional literacy and problem solving are often considered to be awkward, rude, lying, non-compliant, manipulative etc., to quote some labels given. The reality behind these labels is a lot more complex when you think about communication difficulties. CYP who have limited means of understanding and making sense of their own distress may express their internalised distress through anger, violence and self-harm. Resulting effects on mental health can include anxiety disorders, mood disorders, obsessive-compulsive disorders and stress-induced psychosis. Arising from these, CYP may present with a range of high-risk behaviours including violence and aggression towards property, other people and themselves.

'There is a direct correlation between children with a communication disability, and low attainment, behavioural and emotional difficulties, mental health issues, poor employment or training prospects and youth crime. Again, there is a need to do something about these communication difficulties, which is at the start point of the very basis of what we want to do.' (I-Can, Cost to the Nation of Children's Poor Communication, 2006 cited by Lord Ramsbottom to the House of Lords 27/10/2006)

One third of children with developmental language disorders develop mental health problems with resulting criminal involvement in some cases (Clegg *et al*, 1999, cited in Bryan, 2004).

'People with a primary communication need are at greater risk of secondary mental health problems.' (Snowling *et al*, 2006)

Speech and language therapy (SALT) management needs to be an integral part of the appropriate multidisciplinary team, across agencies in most cases (Kramer *et al*, 2008; Scofield *et al*, 2009). Management should encompass behavioural, educational, work and social issues. Specific SALT interventions with those with a primary speech, language or communication need may prevent secondary mental health problems.

Everyday adjustments and supports

Communication is everybody's business. This section aims to give practical advice to enable more effective communication with a child or young person.

Preparation

- Provide the person with information about the appointment/visit before it takes place. Consider including information such as your photo and a visual reference to where the appointment will be.

- Send a list of actions/key points of what will occur or be discussed in a session. If this can be supported with a symbol, photos or drawings this will enable the person to prepare for the session and can also be used as an aid during the appointment.

- Check what AAC systems may be in place before an interaction. Even if a communication partner is not able to use them, being aware of adjustments in place can aid interactions.

Environmental considerations

- Make information accessible.

- Add visual cues – e.g. timetables, labelling areas.

- Minimise distractions – reduce background noise and visual overload.

- Make sure seating is comfortable and supportive.

- Consider individual workstations.

- Have available quiet or safe spaces.

Communication partners

- May require training (home, school, respite).
- Need for family-based interventions.
- Consider holistic needs for additional support – arrange carers assessments.

Top tips/strategies

- Use short, grammatically simple phrases/sentences.
- Use visual cues so the CYP does not have to rely on what they hear. Use signs/gestures, pointing, pictures, symbol boards, drawing etc, as appropriate, to scaffold their understanding.
- Use concrete language ('put the books in the cupboard' **not** 'tidy up').
- Use everyday words (car **not** vehicle).
- Limit complex concepts (time, size, position).
- Allow time for processing and formulating a response. Before repeating or rewording a question, wait and count silently to 10.
- Check understanding before moving on as some people are skilled at hiding their difficulties.
- Monitor facial expression as an indication of whether they understand what you have said.
- CYP are not always able to do two things at the same time (looking at something and listening to people talk about something else).
- Encourage CYP to listen to one person at a time to reduce anxiety.
- Some CYP may take in part of what is said or have difficulties processing long sentences. If you say something differently they have to start processing it again. Repeat sentences/questions exactly the same way before rephrasing.
- Some people will process language more slowly, or may generate language more slowly or have difficulties recalling words. Give them time to process what you have said and tell you what they want to say.
- Use CYP's name when you address them.
- Always tell CYP what you want them to do, **not** what not to do (e.g. 'walk slowly' **not** 'don't run').
- Do not use higher-order language such as sayings and sarcasm; these are easily misinterpreted.
- Spoken language disappears. Use visual supports as these are stationary and can be referred back to.

- Encourage and reward self-monitoring and self-help strategies.
- Accept and value all forms of communication as equally important, e.g. pointing is valued the same as speech.

References

Nind M & Hewett D (2001) *A Practical Guide to Intensive Interaction*. BILD publication, UK.

Bell D & Cameron L (2008) From Dare I say...? to I dare say: a case example illustrating the extension of the use of Talking Mats to people with intellectual disabilities who are able to speak but unwilling to do so. *British Journal of Learning Disability* **36** 122–127.

Murphy J & Cameron L (2008) The effectiveness of Talking Mats for people with intellectual disability. *British Journal of Learning Disability* **36** 232–241.

Gray C & Garand J (1993) *Social Stories: Improving responses of students with autism with accurate information* [online]. Focus on Autistic Behavior. Available at: https://carolgraysocialstories.com/wp-content/uploads/2015/10/Social-Stories-Improving-Responses-of-Students-with-Autism-with-Accurate-Social-Information.pdf (accessed June 2020).

Frost, L., & Bondy, A. (1992, August). *The picture-exchange communication system: An interactive communication system*. Paper presented at the meeting of the International Society for Augmentative and Alternative Communication, Philadelphia, PA.

Bishop DVM (2017) Why is it so hard to reach agreement on terminology? The case of developmental language disorder (DLD). *International Journal of Language and Communication Disorders* **52** (6) 671–680.

Website resources

BILD Fact sheets: www.bild.org.uk/factheets/intensiveinteraction.htm

Communication Matters: https://communicationmatters.org.uk

Makaton website: www.makaton.org

Communication Passports: www.communicationpassports.org.uk

Chapter 8: Occupational therapy

Tina Bang-Andersen

Chapter summary

This chapter explores the role of occupational therapy for children and young people with co-existing intellectual disability and mental health needs. We will look at occupational therapy models and how the models inform occupational therapy assessment and treatment. It looks at various approaches to address occupational participation and minimise challenging behaviours associated with sensory processing challenges, emotional dysregulation and frustration associated with motor co-ordination challenges which are acting as barriers to engagement in meaningful occupations.

Introduction

Performance of self-care and daily living tasks are essential to a child's independence but are often delayed in children with coexisting learning disability and mental health needs (Bal *et al*, 2015; Jasmin *et al*, 2009; Case-Smith & Clifford O'Brien, 2015). Examples of skills that are particularly difficult to master include toileting, dressing, personal hygiene and eating. Children with disabilities are more likely to have restricted participation in home, school and community activities, and in creating positive social relationships.

Children with disabilities have poor coping strategies and are more likely to disengage from stressful situations. Challenges to engage in meaningful occupations and associated occupational performance difficulties, barriers to independence, sensory dysregulation and poor social engagement with peers and engagement with activities in the local community cause high levels of frustration, stress and anxiety. This can impact emotional regulation and can further exacerbate challenging behaviours associated with intellectual disability and mental health. Many children and young people with developmental delays, autism spectrum disorder, and/or attention deficit hyperactivity disorder (ADHD) experience significant sensory integration difficulties which impacts on daily life and behaviour (Ayres, 1979; Smith Roley *et al*, 2001).

Some families may experience their child's disability positively (Blacher & Baker, 2007; Hastings *et al*, 2005) where other families report negative consequences which can include disruption in family routines and to activities (Mactavish & Schleien, 2004) as well as a strained ability to provide effective care (Kogan *et al*, 2008). Parents report that barriers to participation are poor access to environment; the physical cognitive and social demands of an activity; and attitudes and safety. Occupational therapists working with children with learning disability play an integral role in addressing occupational performance challenges and in assisting the child/young person to participate in their daily roles.

Occupational therapy in learning disability with mental health needs

Occupational therapy is a person-centred approach that promotes a balanced range of occupations to enhance health and well-being, where 'occupations' refers to everything people do in their daily lives. Children learn and develop through their participation in activities and occupations (Lane *et al*, 2012) and play is an essential occupation of childhood, from which children develop language, self-regulation and problem-solving skills (Lifter *et al*, 2011). Occupations can also include:

- Self-care e.g. getting dressed, eating a meal, washing, toileting and sleeping.
- Being productive e.g. participating in nursery or school, doing chores.
- Leisure e.g. socialising with friends, belonging to a group, participating in hobbies.

(Royal College of Occupational Therapists, 2016)

Children and young people engage in many social and occupational roles every day. Typically developing children engage in occupations relevant to these roles throughout their daily life such playing, getting dressed, eating, engaging in household chores and school work tasks, as well as leisure activities such as football, dance or playing an instrument. Children engage in these occupations in various environments such as at home, at school, at friend's homes and in their local communities such as at leisure centres, parks and churches. Csikszentmihalyi (1993) evidenced that people experience the most enjoyment in their lives when they are actively engaged in meaningful activity. Occupational therapists are committed to help people engage in meaningful and enjoyable occupations to promote health and well-being.

Occupational therapists believe that everyone has the right to obtain their full potential. Children with a disability may therefore come in contact with an occupational therapist when there are concerns about their occupational performance due to illness, injury, disability or mental health which is impacting on their ability to engage with meaningful roles, perform tasks or activities, or which is creating environmental barriers to performance and participation.

Theory and practice models used by occupational therapists

There are a number of theories, models of practice, frames of reference and interventions that may be used with children and young people with coexisting mental health issues and learning disability.

The literature recommends that occupational therapists create their own 'multimodel' to meet an individual's needs due to the complexity of children with a learning disability (Nelson, 2009). It is important to formulate consistent and clear models of practice, frames of reference and intervention planning for children and young people with a learning disability and mental health needs and there is a sparse evidence base for occupational therapy intervention in child and adolescent mental health services (Harrison & Forsyth, 2005).

Overarching models in occupational therapy

Using theory, assessment and clinical reasoning, occupational therapists hypothesise and develop interventions to improve occupational performance and participation of children (Case-Smith & Clifford O'Brien, 2015) based on the goals identified with the child and/or family.

Below are two of the main models that guide the gathering of information about the child/young person.

Model of Human Occupation (MOHO)

The Model of Human Occupation (MOHO) is currently the most widely used theory in occupational therapy research and practice (Haglund *et al*, 2000). MOHO is a conceptual framework and practical tool to guide assessment, clinical reasoning, effect change, and measure the impact of interventions. It guides occupational therapists to consider the personal values and interests, roles and responsibilities and environmental contexts of each child (Kielhofner, 2008). MOHO is complementary to practice that is based on other occupational therapy models and interdisciplinary theories, and therefore embraces the 'multimodel' approach.

Canadian Model of Occupational Performance (CMOP)

The Canadian Model of Occupational Performance (CMOP) is a social model that places the child in a social-environmental context and is an interactive model exploring the relationship between the person, their roles and their environment. In this model, self-care, productivity and leisure are considered key components of occupation. The model invites other models into the performance components which are affective, physical and cognitive (Sumsion, 2006).

Occupation and child/family-centred approach

Both MOHO and CMOP enables the occupational therapist to engage the child and family in occupation-centred practice by focusing on occupations and the environment during the assessment and treatment process (Rodgers, 2010). Child-centred practice must be meaningful to the child and family, which means that the child and family are active participants in all stages of the process. A trusting and collaborative partnership needs to be developed through active engagement, fostering motivation and commitment.

Occupational therapists use a number of strategies to foster the partnership with the child and their family:

- Creating choices.
- Individualised treatment, including child and family chosen goals.
- Structuring success.
- Exchanging stories.
- Joint problem-solving.
- Ensuring developmental, cultural and gender appropriateness.

(Rodgers, 2010, p29)

Occupational therapy process

Occupational therapists are guided by the occupational therapy process, which includes the following steps:

Information gathering – this process focuses on the child's occupational and social roles, occupations and the environmental context for performance.

Assessment – this process identifies the child's occupation and environment that either facilitates or impedes occupational performance using various standardised assessment tools and clinical observations to inform the goal-setting process and treatment process.

Goal setting – goals are set based on the child's and family's priorities of what occupations are meaningful and how they fit into the context of family life. This is crucial for motivating the child and supporting the ability of the parents to achieve the goals.

Intervention – an intervention is put in place based on the identified goals that emphasises skills acquisition, modifying occupations/tasks and/or the environment, and modifying behaviour to support the person to engage in meaningful and purposeful occupation.

Evaluation of intervention – outcome measures are used that consider occupational performance, roles, habits, values and participation.

Assessment tools used in the assessment process

The Model of Human Occupation (MOHO) has various assessment tools that may be appropriate to use in the assessment process to determine which occupations are meaningful and purposeful to the child. The assessment tools capture a child's strengths and challenges irrespective of symptoms, diagnosis, age, or the treatment setting.

The SCOPE and COSA are useful initial assessment tools in the meeting with the child and parent(s) to understand their occupational competencies, performance and current occupational balance. They give insights into what is important and meaningful to the child and how to ensure occupational goal setting is motivating for the child as well as realistic for them within the context of the family structure.

Short Child Occupational Profile (SCOPE)

The SCOPE assesses factors that represent the MOHO concepts of volition, habituation, performance capacity and the environment. It identifies areas which need further assessment and directs the practitioner to complimentary paediatric assessments in order to gain an increased understanding of specific barriers to occupational participation (Bowyer *et al*, 2006).

Child Occupational Self Assessment (COSA)

The COSA is a child-directed assessment tool and outcome measure that captures the child's or young person's perceptions of their occupational competencies and the importance they place on everyday activities across home, school and community (Keller *et al*, 2006).

Based on the findings using the Model of Human Occupation, further standardised assessments may be used to understand occupational barriers. The standardised paediatric assessment tools developed for children mainly focus on the developmental domains of gross motor skills, fine motor skills, visual motor/visual-perceptual skills, motor and process skills and sensory processing.

The most common assessment tools are:

- Miller Function & Participation Scale (M-FUN)
- Bruininks-Oseretsky Test of Motor Proficiency (2nd ed) (BOT-2)
- Sensory Integration Praxis Tests (SIPT)
- Sensory Profile (SP)
- Adolescent/Adult Sensory profile (AASP)
- Sensory Processing Measure (SPM)
- Assessment of Motor and Process Skills (AMPS)

(Richardson, 2015)

Child-centred interventions in occupational therapy

As previously described, occupational therapists use a 'multimodel' when engaging in the assessment and treatment process in which they draw from a range of different models and frames of references to guide clinical reasoning and treatment planning.

Copley *et al* (2008) postulates that occupational therapists create their own 'theory of practice'. At times, therapists will use pure approaches such as Ayres Sensory Integration (ASI), but more often they will use a combination of intervention approaches and tailor these to the unique needs of each child, family and service context. This flexibility and adaptability of the occupational therapist places them in a strong position to work with children and young people with various challenges as a result of mental health and intellectual disability.

Occupational therapists use teaching and coaching of parents and teachers, which is led by the professional with pre-planned information to share. Occupational Performance coaching is a collaborative process to help parents develop awareness, knowledge and skills that enable and empower them to design their own solutions to meet the child's needs. Occupational performance coaching focuses specifically on the enablement of children and parents' participation in occupations in home and community contexts through parent-identified solutions to performance barriers (Graham *et al*, 2009; King *et al*, 2017).

Teaching and coaching often occurs as a dynamic process where parents and teachers commonly express relief at:

- understanding puzzling and frustrating behaviours
- understanding they have not caused the problem
- having a greater appreciation of the challenges their child faces.

Sensory integration therapy

'Sensory integration is the organisation of sensation for use' (Ayres, 1979, p5) and is the foundation for adaptive responses to challenges imposed by the environment and learning (Spitzer & Smith Roley, 2001).

It is estimated that 70-90% of children with autism may have sensory related difficulties. Children with ADHD have been reported to have difficulties in all areas of sensory modulation. Evidence suggests that individuals with intellectual disabilities and pervasive developmental disorders have atypical sensory processing which may contribute to self-stimulatory and self-injurious behaviour. When people experience deficits with sensory processing and integration they struggle with performing everyday occupations, which impacts on participation in activities within the home, school and the community (Case-Smith & Arbesman, 2008; NICE guidelines 2008).

Sensory processing is the brain's ability to receive, register, organise and interpret sensory information. These processes are important for adaptive behaviour, which means actions such as play, activities of daily living, learning, behaviour and social participation. Neuroplasticity is considered the key postulate on which sensory integration is based.

Children with ASD and ADHD have been found to exhibit motor planning deficits and poor praxis, in particular ideational praxis. Ayres (1989) described praxis as '...the ability by which an individual learns to use his or her hands and body in a skilled task. Practice skills is fundamental to purposeful activity ... It involves an internal program of ideation...' (p9).

The child-centered approach most frequently used with children diagnosed with ASD is sensory integration therapy (Thompson-Hodgetts & Magill-Evans, 2018).

Ayres Sensory Integration (ASI)

ASI intervention is an individualised occupational therapy approach in which the therapist organises activities to improve sensory integration capacities with a view to improving occupational performance in daily life. Ayres originally designed

ASI for children with learning disabilities, but it is now being used for a range of disabilities including autism, ADHD and fragile-X syndrome.

Sensory stimulation protocols

These are interventions that entail specific types of sensory stimulation that are managed by the therapist and delivered in a predetermined manner with a view to improve sensory modulation, self-regulation, language development, attention and learning. Examples include:

- Wilbarger Protocol, which is a touch pressure programme brushing the skin followed by compression of specific joints.
- Astronaut Program, which applies rotary vestibular sensation combined with sound stimulation.
- Therapeutic Listening Program/QuickShift, which is a sound-based program using headphones or other listening systems to stimulate neuroplasticity.

Sensory-based strategies

Sensory-based strategies are sensory interventions with flexible guidelines for use in daily life and are mainly administered by a parent, teacher or by the child. Examples of the most researched are:

- wearing weighted vests for touch-pressure and enhanced proprioception
- sitting on a therapy ball for vestibular-proprioceptive input
- using body-compression devices such as the Grandin hug machine.

Other sensory-based strategies that are frequently used are:

Sensory diet, which is a strategy for developing home-and school-based programmes that target an individual's need for specific sensory experiences, enhancing occupational performance for the child.

Sensory circuits, which is a strategy that encourages children to participate in a series of motor activities with the aim of enhancing attention and concentration in readiness for the day's learning. It can also enhance sensory processing abilities over time.

The Alert Program for Self-Regulation is designed to improve awareness of self-regulation through charts, worksheets and activities using sensory strategies to self-regulate.

Consultation on modification of activities, routines and environment

This approach aims at managing sound, light, smells, visual distraction and other people. This could be wearing ear defenders, minimising visual distractors in class, allowing child to eat in classroom rather than lunch hall etc.

Other intervention approaches

Cognitive Orientation for Daily Occupational Performance (COOP)

Cognitive Orientation for Daily Occupational Performance (COOP) is an occupation-child centred intervention that enhances children's skill acquisition, enables engagement in relevant occupations and therefore promotes participation in activities of daily life. COOP was originally developed for children with developmental co-ordination disorder (DCD). The approach has subsequently been used and researched with a variety of populations including those with Asperger's syndrome.

Perceive, Recall, Plan and Perform (PRPP)

Perceive, recall, plan and perform (PRPP) is an occupation-centred task analysis and intervention system in which the following are considered: the processing capacity of the child, the processing demands of the task, and the processing demands of the context of performance. The application of strategies is observed during every day tasks such as buttoning a shirt, and strategies are taught within the context of the task to improve performance.

Motor learning and skill acquisition

Motor learning as a model of practice focuses on supporting the child to achieve goal-directed functional actions. Motor learning is an occupation-based approach because it is a search for a motor solution which emerges from an interaction between the child and the task and the environment.

Forward/backward chaining

The Chaining approach breaks down an activity into small parts (a chain), which are then taught step-by-step in the correct sequence, frequently by modelling parts of the chain. Forward chaining is teaching the first steps of the chain to complete the activity, and backwards chaining teaches the last steps first. Backwards chaining can be more motivating for the child as they can observe an instant result. Visual pictures of the sequence are often used to support the learning process and can be used in the environment subsequently as prompts.

Conclusion

The occupational therapy process informs an understanding of occupational performance and participation and what is meaningful and important to the child or young person. Understanding their motivation is essential for occupational engagement with a view to addressing any barriers that cause frustration and anxiety.

Sensory integration difficulties may be a barrier to engagement as children and young people with mental health needs and learning difficulties frequently struggle with sensory modulation and motor co-ordination difficulties. Implementing strategies to address these sensory integration difficulties becomes vital when addressing behaviour, anxiety, learning and activities of daily living.

References

Arbesman M, Bazyk S & Nochajski SM (2013) Systematic review of occupational therapy and mental health promotion, prevention, and intervention for children and youth. *American Journal of Occupational Therapy* **67** (6) e120-e130. doi: 10.5014/ajot.2013.008359.

Ayres AJ (1979) *Sensory Integration and the child.* Los Angeles: Western Psychological Services.

Ayres AJ (1989) *Sensory Integration and Praxis Test (SIPT) Manual.* Los Angeles: Western Psychological Services.

Bal VH, Kim SH, Cheong D & Lord C (2015) Daily living skills in individuals with autism spectrum disorder from 2 to 21 years of age. *Autism* **19** 774–784.

Bazyk S & Arbesman M (2013) *Occupational Therapy Practice Guidelines for Mental Health Promotion, Prevention, and Intervention for Children and Youth.* Bethesda, MD: AOTA Press.

Blacher J & Baker BL (2007) Positive impact of intellectual disability on families. *American Journal of Mental Retardation* **112** 330–348.

Braveman B, Fisher G, Suarez-Balcazar Y (2010) Achieving the Ordinary Things: A tribute to Gary Kielhofner. *The American Journal of Occupational Therapy* **64** (6) 828–831

Bowyer P, Kramer J, Ploszaj A *et al.* (2006) *The Short Child Occupational Profile (SCOPE).* Version 2.2. The University of Illinois at Chicago.

Bundy AC & Murray EA (2002) *Sensory Integration: A Jean Ayres' theory revisited.* In: AC Bundy, SJ Lane, EA Murray (Eds.) *Sensory Integration: Theory and practice.* 2nd Edition. F.A. Company. Philadelphia. Pp3–33.

Case-Smith J & Arbesman M (2008) Evidence-based review of intervention for autism used in or relevant to occupational therapy. *American Journal of Occupational Therapy* **62** (3) 462–473.

Copley J, Nelson A, Turpin M, Underwood K & Flanigan K (2008) Factors influencing therapist's interventions for children with learning difficulties. *Canadian Journal of Occupational therapy* **75** (2) pp. 105-113.

Csikszentmihalyi M (1993). Activity and happiness: Towards a science of occupation. *Journal of Occupational Science* **1** 38–42. http://dx.doi.org/10.1080/14427591.1993.9686377

Graham F, Rodger S & Ziviani J (2009) Coaching parents to enable children's participation: An approach for working with parents and their children. *Australian Occupational Therapy Journal* **56** 16-23.

Haglund l, Ekbladh E, Thorell LH & and Halberg I (2000) Practice models in Swedish psychiatric occupational therapy. *Scandinavian Journal of Occupational Therapy* **7** 107-113.

Hastings RP, Beck A & Hill C (2005) Positive contributions made by children with an intellectual disability in the family: Mothers' and fathers' perceptions. *Journal of Intellectual Disabilities* **9** 155–165.

Jasmin E, Couture M, McKinley P, Reid G, Fombonne E & Gisel E (2009) Sensori-motor and daily living skills of preschool children with autism spectrum disorders. *Journal of Autism and Developmental Disorders* **39** 231–241.

Keller J, Kafkes A, Basu S, Federico J & Kilehofner G (2006) *Child Occupational Self Assessment (COSA)* Version 2.1. The University of Illinois at Chicago.

King G, Williams L & Hahn Goldberg S (2017) Family- oriented services in pediatric rehabilitation: A scoping review and framework to promote parent and family wellness. *Child: Care, Health and Development* **43** 334–347.

Kogan MD, Strickland BB, Blumberg SJ, Singh GK, Perrin JM & van Dyck PC (2008) A national profile of the health care experiences and family impact of autism spectrum disorder among children in the United States, 2005–2006. *Pediatrics* **122**, e1149–e1158.

Lane SJ, Reynolds S & Dumenci L (2012) Sensory overresponsivity and anxiety in typically developing children and children with autism and attention deficit hyperactivity disorder: Cause or coexistence? *American Journal of Occupational Therapy* **66** (5) pp595-603.

Lifter K, Foster-Sanda S, Arzamarski C, Briesch J & McClure E (2011) Overview of play: Its uses and importance in early intervention/early childhood special education. *Infants and Young Children* **24** 225–245.

Mactavish JB & Schleien SJ (2004). Re-injecting spontaneity and balance in family life: Parents' perspectives on recreation in families that include children with developmental disability. *Journal of Intellectual Disability Research* **48** 123–141.

National Institute for Health ad Care Excellence (2008) (last modified: March 2013) *CH72: Attention Deficit Hyperactivity Disorder: Diagnosis and management of ADHD in children, young people and adults.*

Richardson PK (2015) Use of standardized tests in pediatric practice. In: J Case-Smith & J Clifford O'Brien. Eds: *Occupational therapy for Children and Adolescent*. Elsevier Mosby.

Rodgers S (2010). *Occupation-Centred Practice with Children: A practical guide for occupational therapists*. Whiley-Blackwell.

Royal College of Occupational Therapy (2015) *Occupational Therapy for Children and Young People.*

Royal College of Occupational Therapy (April 2016) *Provision and commissioning of Occupational Therapy Services for Children and Young People.*

Smith Roley S, Blanche EI & Schaaf RC (2001) *Sensory Integration with Diverse Population*. Texas: Pro-ed.

Smith Roley S, Blanche EI & Schaaf RC. Eds. *Client-centred practice in occupational therapy*. Churchill Livingstone Elsevier. Pp. 147-159.

Sumsion T (2006) *Client-centred Practice in Occupational Therapy: A guide to Implementation*. 2nd Edition. Churchill Livingstone Elsevier.

Thompson-Hodgetts S & Magill-Evans J (2018) Sensory-Based Approaches in Intervention for Children With Autism Spectrum Disorder: Influences on Occupational Therapists' Recommendations and Perceived Benefits. *American Journal of Occupational Therapy* **72** (3).

Section 3:
Interventions
and services

Chapter 9: Psychological interventions

Dr Ruksana Ahmed

Chapter summary

This chapter provides an update on psychological approaches for working with children and young people with intellectual disabilities. Overall, psychological approaches to working with children and young people with intellectual disabilities remain similar to the approaches used with children and young people that experience mental health difficulties without intellectual disabilities. However, there are key factors and skills required that will increase the likelihood of effectiveness when working with children and young people with intellectual disabilities. For example, families continue to need to be engaged and their expert knowledge of their child valued; diagnoses and formulations need to be explained in ways that are meaningful; differences of opinion within the family, and perhaps with professionals, continue to require negotiation; and interventions should ideally be offered to individuals, families and groups. In addition to these key factors, this chapter also provides updates about common therapeutic approaches used with children and young people with intellectual disabilities and highlights the adaptations necessary from generic interventions and approaches. Psychoeducation, behavioural, cognitive behaviour and group approaches are considered, with additional consideration given to interventions and approaches aimed towards children and young people with autistic spectrum disorder.

Introduction

Before considering any approaches and skills for working with children and young people with intellectual disabilities and mental health difficulties, key challenges must be considered and accepted by mental health professionals.

First, there should be an acknowledgement that the available evidence-based interventions will require adaptation to the child/young person's (CYP) strengths and deficits. Second, mental health professionals will be required to ensure that parents'/carers' and professionals' expectations of the effectiveness of interventions and outcomes are appropriate considering the child or young person's developmental and chronological age.

Consideration and acceptance of these challenges can then allow for the use of modified approaches and interventions. Any such approaches and interventions will also require supplementation with teams, networks and agencies. Key agencies will include education and social care so that liaison and approaches can be applied across different environments and contexts. It remains fundamental that, where possible, parents and carers continue to be co-therapists and a model of genuine collaboration with families is maintained. This collaboration will allow for successful modifications of established behavioural, cognitive behavioural and parenting interventions and approaches.

Framework for interventions

There remains a dearth of evidence regarding the effectiveness of psychological interventions with children and young people with intellectual disabilities. This is in part because of the heterogeneous nature of these children and young people, which challenges the ability to design, conduct and interpret studies. It is also suggested that, as there are established evidence-based interventions for children and young people with mental health difficulties without intellectual disabilities, it is these approaches that should be applied in modified versions. For children and young people with intellectual disabilities, it is important to motivate them and make sure they understand interventions. Moreover, their understanding and motivation will be impacted by that of their parents or caregivers. Therefore, the emotional capacity and social circumstances of parents and carers, combined with the CYP's cognitive and functional skills, will be requirements of a framework for effective interventions and approaches.

The following factors are essential requirements of such frameworks:

- The CYP's emotional and developmental age should guide the selection of intervention.

- Adaptations should be made in line with the CYP's individual communication, cognitive and adaptive skills and needs.

- Evidence-based interventions are of relevance once modified to incorporate process factors.

- Evidence-based interventions for children and young people without intellectual disabilities are often delivered as systemic interventions, and these requirements should not therefore prevent similar delivery to children and young people with intellectual disabilities.

Family engagement

The importance of carers and families as collaborators cannot be emphasised enough and will often be a key factor in determining the effectiveness of interventions and approaches for children and young people with intellectual disabilities. However, when barriers to collaboration arise, these can often be mis-attributed to poor parent/carer motivation. It is important to consider parental cognitive and emotional development and parental intellectual disabilities and mental health difficulties when planning interventions and approaches. It is imperative that these factors are considered constructively and unconditionally, to prevent parents and carers being perceived as the sole contributors to the CYP's difficulties.

It is also widely recognised that family structures and constellations have changed from historic constructs. Therefore, clinicians and professionals must utilise frameworks that have the ability to be flexible to the changing structures and constructs of families today as well as in the future.

Psychoeducation

There remain two key aspects to using psychoeducation as an effective approach with children and young people with intellectual disabilities. For the individual child or young person, parent/carer and professional, this approach can inform an understanding of an individual's profile, including strengths and difficulties. In addition to this, psychoeducation can form the basis for teaching and training in an identified area e.g. developing social skills, managing funds etc.

Developing an appropriate understanding of diagnosis in a meaningful fashion for children and young people with intellectual disabilities is essential in order to contribute to the development of a positive sense of identity and a reduction in stigma from care providers.

Psychoeducation can also be a significant aid in dynamic interventions that are tailored. The following are examples of a range of therapeutic areas of need that can be successfully targeted:

- Parents/carers who are experiencing difficulties managing the impact of their child's intellectual disabilities may set unrealistic expectations for their child and themselves, with significant emotional and behavioural consequences.
- Parents/carers may have a different understanding of their child's intellectual disabilities, which could in turn contribute to less effective intervention outcomes.

- Children and young people with intellectual disabilities may become more behaviourally and emotionally vulnerable in the context of more limited understanding of their own strengths and difficulties.

Overall, there are numerous examples of how psychoeducation can play a significant role as an approach, and within the context of effective interventions for children and young people with intellectual disabilities.

Skills teaching and training

Psychologists can also use psychoeducation for the purpose of skills teaching and training. Areas that can be taught can include emotional literacy training, social skills training and education about the nature of social and sexual relationships. It is often recommended that this type of training takes place in a school setting, but if a more individual approach is needed due to the nature of behavioural presentation or poor response to such an intervention and associated mental health difficulties, then a psychologist can design and implement an appropriate individual intervention.

Children and young people with intellectual disabilities will often experience difficulties with social interactions and peer relationships. These difficulties can often become more prevalent and impairing during the middle years of childhood, and contributing factors can include the impact of impaired language skills, difficulties in social and emotional reciprocity, impulsivity and a lack of understanding of social nuances and rules. The consequences for children and young people can be significant, with experiences of isolation, social exclusion and loss of established peer relationships. In turn, these experiences can have further negative consequences for the mental health of children and young people. Therefore, social skills teaching and training can contribute to reducing some of these difficulties.

Social skills teaching and training can be offered at either individual or group levels, both for children and young people with and without autism spectrum disorder, and may be offered at school or as a clinic-based intervention. There are a range of intervention packages that have been developed and evaluated (Kavale & Mostert, 2004; Leaf et al, 2017). These interventions include training in social problem solving, friendships and conversation planning, and dealing with feelings. More specifically, these areas may include teaching specific skills including: starting a conversation, asking questions, listening to others, expressing your feelings, negotiating, apologising, dealing with frustration or anger, or making decisions. A range of techniques are used in this process, such as direct instruction, modelling, coaching, rehearsal, shaping, prompting and reinforcement

(Kavale & Mostert, 2004; Leaf *et al*, 2017). Although overall subsequent analysis and reviews of social skills training have reported poor long-terms outcomes and small effect sizes, participants and teachers and parents have reported finding training 'beneficial'. There remains an argument for continued development of such interventions and their systematic evaluation in order to ascertain the potential benefits to children and young people with intellectual disabilities with and without autism spectrum disorder.

Further evidence of such need becomes evident when considering the high prevalence of experiences of bullying and victimisation for children and young people with intellectual disabilities with and without autism spectrum disorder. Using techniques such as role-play to demonstrate skills and reduce symptoms of anxiety could contribute positively to both avoidance and management of negative peer interactions and relationships. In addition to this, at a systemic level, considering wider community access to leisure activities and vocational and occupational opportunities as a result of social skills teaching and training could lead to more optimal and sustained skills acquisition and outcomes.

Another area of significant importance for children and young people with intellectual disabilities is that of sexual development and the associated behaviours and appropriate relationships. Overall, this area of need is common, however it increases in relevance and importance following puberty. In adolescence, a lack of understanding and awareness can make young people with intellectual disabilities vulnerable to abuse and exploitation. Although these vulnerabilities have always been present, the proliferation of the use of technology (internet and social media) by children and young people and by potential abusers has led to an exponential increase in vulnerabilities and associated risks.

Therefore, although the areas of need remain similar, such as supporting young people to understand sexual development and to provide information about appropriate and inappropriate behaviours and consent, these also need to be considered in the context of technological environments which children and young people regularly access. Associated risks remain of young people being misjudged as potential instigators of intentional inappropriate behaviours, when they are actually engaging in such behaviours without the understanding of highly complex constructs and situations. In these circumstances, psychoeducation packages could prove extremely useful in teaching young people with intellectual disabilities. Such interventions will inevitably need to ensure that the technological environments are incorporated and specific skills and strategies are provided to manage these developing environments.

Behavioural approaches

It still remains true that the most common presenting difficulties in children and young people with intellectual disabilities include behaviours such as physical or verbal aggression, oppositionality, stereotypical behaviours or sexualised behaviour. These behaviours can be more or less challenging in nature for children and young people, parents/carers and professionals. Often, but not exclusively, these behaviours can pose more challenges when they arise in contexts outside of the home. More often, these behaviours can be present and impairing across multiple contexts. Evidence continues to indicate that the most effective approaches and interventions are behavioural. There is also continuing evidence of the effectiveness of behavioural approaches for a wide variety of difficulties relating to attention, anxiety and conduct in children and young people without identified intellectual disabilities (Fonagy et al, 2015). Therefore, there remains a case for using behavioural approaches for co-occurring difficulties in children and young people who have a range of intellectual disabilities including mild, moderate, severe or profound disabilities.

When considering behavioural approaches, these can be considered as standardised parental interventions and individually designed and delivered interventions.

Parent training interventions

There is a number of effective and established group parent training interventions that target children and young people who access mental health services. These interventions aim to 'train' parents to understand their child's behaviour, and to learn techniques to manage identified behaviours. Many of these established interventions have been modified and used with parents of children and young people with intellectual disabilities.

For parents, a key positive factor is that such interventions can provide contact with many other parents at the same time, increasing their social support through developing relationships within the group. The evidence suggests that both generic parent training interventions as well as those modified specifically for use with parents of children with intellectual disabilities can be effective (Beresford, 2009). Further evaluation is required to compare the relative effectiveness of generic and modified interventions. Clinicians continue to posit that the level of cognitive and functional impairment may contribute to the effectiveness of such interventions and there remains an 'anecdotal' argument for increased modifications in the context of increasing impairment across domains. There are limited evaluations comparing group and individual interventions in relation to increased effectiveness, and parents and carers continue to express preferences for groups and individual interventions.

Established manualised interventions continue to be used across early years and adolescence (Webster-Stratton, 2001; Sanders *et al*, 2001). These interventions draw on behavioural principles and focus on techniques such as the selective ignoring of undesirable behaviour, alongside the use of praise, attention and other rewards to increase desired behaviour in order to alter parent-child interaction patterns, along with the judicious use of 'time-outs' for behaviours that cannot be ignored. Adaptations to these generic programmes may include using developmentally appropriate strategies rather than focusing on chronological age; encouraging parents to identify more relevant clinical presentations, which include learning and developmental difficulties; excluding using 'time-out' and replacing it with methods to predict and avoid, or reduce frequency and severity of incidents; identify potential reinforcers and adapted reward systems and techniques that take into account developmental and functional levels of children and young people (McIntyre, 2008).

Individualised Behavioural Interventions

When individualised behavioural interventions are required, it is important that they are built upon robust functional analysis of behaviours that are being considered for intervention. For more intractable behaviour problems, an individual approach based on functional analysis of the behaviours will be necessary. A robust functional analysis will allow for data to be collected about environmental factors, trigger stimuli and reinforcers. This will then allow for both proactive and preventative strategies to be considered. The same methodology will also allow for reactive strategies to be established in order to de-escalate and manage behaviours once they occur. The core principles of Emerson (2001), stating that any interventions to modify behaviour must be constructional, functional and socially valid, remain as fundamental today as ever when working with children and young people with intellectual disabilities:

- **Constructional** – Intervention must aim to teach new skills and not just focus on 'eliminating' behaviours.
- **Functional** – Intervention must be informed by accurate analysis of the function of the behaviour being modified.
- **Social validity** – Intervention must be meaningful and purposeful to the CYP and parents and carers with improvement to quality of life, participation and opportunities.

When considering preventative strategies, these are more likely to involve modifying the environment to avoid triggers to the behaviour and also to teach new skills to help the child or young person to cope with the triggers that cannot be modified. Overall, supporting the learning of coping skills is always required as there can be many environments and situations that cannot be significantly modified. Learning new skills can also allow for increased opportunities.

Specific examples of areas of intervention and preventative strategies and interventions can include:

- improving sleep patterns using behavioural approaches
- using desensitisation and graded exposure techniques across domains
- use of visual schedules and structured activity scheduling
- appropriate use of preferred activities
- increase in social reinforcers and rewards
- skills acquisition and development appropriate to cognitive and functional abilities.

When considering behaviours that are challenging, two approaches are regarded as most effective. The first is to consider behaviours that challenge in relation to their communicative purpose. In these circumstances, functional communication training allows for 'new' and more appropriate behaviours to be identified and taught. This is turn results in the 'new' behaviour being more effective socially (Carr *et al*, 1994; Johnston *et al*, 2006). The effectiveness of such an approach can be optimised by implementing it in a systemic fashion and using expertise across disciplines. This can allow for the following specific techniques to be used more successfully:

- Incorporating speech and language therapists to teach appropriate communication systems e.g. the Picture Exchange Communication System (PECS), Makaton.
- Ensuring that a wide range of communication systems including those assisted by technology are available with ease for children and young people who may require them.
- The use of flashcards, or other indicators, to allow a child or young person to leave a situation in which they are having difficulty in order to prevent or reduce the propensity for behaviours to deteriorate.
- Joint working with occupational therapists to ensure that sensory assessments and profiles of children and young people are being assessed and incorporated into individualised interventions.

In addition to the communication approach, a second approach to consider is to target in a direct or indirect fashion the reinforcement contingencies that may be operating. For example, a child or young person can be receiving a reinforcer/reward when presenting with desired behaviours. For this method to be effective, the time frame of using reinforcers is a key factor – they must be used in a rapid fashion and consistently across contexts. Some children and young people with intellectual disabilities will respond to 'logical and meaningful consequences'. However, these interventions have been reported to be less effective in response to more severe behaviours that challenge.

As stated previously, for children and young people with intellectual disabilities, some traditional behavioural interventions when used in isolation, whether part of individual and/or parenting interventions, can be less helpful and at times detrimental. These include variations of extinction of behaviours and the use of 'time-out'. Alternatives to such interventions should be considered in order to prevent further immediate and/or delayed detrimental impact.

Cognitive behavioural approaches

It is widely agreed that cognitive behavioural therapy (CBT) is the treatment of choice for a wide variety of mental health conditions in children and adolescents without intellectual disability (Fonagy *et al*, 2015). In addition to this, an adapted package for adults with intellectual disabilities has been developed, although the effectiveness of such interventions remains contingent on verbal abilities (Wilner, 2005). The evidence for the effectiveness of CBT with children and young people with intellectual disabilities remains more limited, however it is more widely agreed that such interventions require greater emphasis on behavioural components and techniques and adaptations:

- Children and young people with intellectual disabilities will always require assessment for suitability for modified CBT.

- Focus on targeting cognitive thoughts, distortions and patterns of thinking, as precipitating and maintaining factors may either not be feasible options or be less constructive.

- Behavioural techniques such a relaxation and sensory based anxiety management techniques will be effective. Such effectiveness is likely to be optimised further by supporting parents/carers and professionals working with children and young people to learn and replicate these techniques across contexts.

- Self-instruction following identification of behavioural indications of cognitive distress may be more effective as a modification for children and young people with intellectual disabilities.

- Minimising the dependency on highly developed verbal communication may allow for children and young people with more significant communication disabilities to use strategies (Dagnan *et al*, 2000).

- Parents/carers as co-therapists is a fundamental modification and its value cannot be emphasised enough.

- Modifications should aim to reduce the use of abstract concepts or, where possible, conversion of these to more 'concrete' and accessible concepts.

- Clinicians will need to model and offer appropriate behaviours, 'cognitions' and solutions more proactively as part of modified interventions.

- Typical CBT visual aids and resources are likely to remain effective and should continue to be used e.g. feelings thermometers, traffic lights etc. Providing children and young people and parents/carers with session content will help with the acquisition of skills and increase the potential for generalisation of skills.

- When pre-requisite cognitive skills are assessed as present then children and young people with intellectual disabilities may be able to access CBT in a similar fashion to children without intellectual disabilities. Careful continued and dynamic assessment of responses to modified interventions will be required.

- Common issues that will continue to require consideration include the structure of sessions, the use of shorter sessions, modifying the pace of sessions and reducing the presence and/or impact of children and young people acquiescing.

Autism spectrum condition specific approaches

A range of autism spectrum condition (ASC) specific interventions exist that aim to remediate core communication and learning deficits through early intervention. Although these programmes have modifications, they also incorporate the behavioural approaches as outlined above, with additional elements of communication training both for the child and parent. Previously identified limitations to research remain, and approaches that are based on applied behaviour analysis (Howlin *et al*, 2009) are among the most thoroughly researched. These programmes recommend that intervention starts before three years of age and should involve approximately 40 hours of intensive home-based behavioural intervention for at least two years. Initial studies reported marked gains in IQ and other skills that led to reintegration to mainstream education (Lovaas, 1987), yet closer consideration of the results shows a wide range of individual results and difficulty in replicating the intensity of the intervention in practice (Howlin *et al*, 2009). Recent meta-analyses by Howlin *et al* (2009) and Eldevik *et al* (2009) conclude that there is good evidence that early and intensive behavioural intervention is effective, but there is wide variability in responses to treatment and, at present, it is unclear what factors influence these responses. A number of other less intensive interventions that target specific skills such as communication or joint social interaction have also been found to be effective in improving the particular skills they target, and further research is required comparing the outcomes of high and low intensity treatments (Howlin *et al*, 2009).

Cognitive behavioural approaches for children and young people with autism spectrum disorder

When considering children and young people with intellectual disabilities and autism spectrum conditions (ASC), the modified cognitive behavioural approaches discussed above are also likely to be useful for increasing the accessibility and potential effectiveness of interventions for children with ASC and intellectual disabilities. There are further modified approaches and interventions that have been specifically developed for children and young people with ASC without intellectual disabilities, and consideration of these modifications may also prove effective (Sofronoff & Attwood, 2003; Attwood *et al*, 2007; Scarpa *et al*, 2013).

In addition to modifications already discussed, incorporation and utilisation of special interests to optimise therapeutic engagement and continued use of special interests as reinforcers could be considered. Another modification to consider is the use of *Social Stories* (Gray, 1995), an autism-specific intervention strategy that is widely used. This approach provides a structured means of teaching expected behaviours in particular situations through developing short stories that describe the relevant situational cues, other people's thoughts, feelings and behaviour, and gives directive statements to teach the young person how to respond appropriately. There is a lack of empirical research into this approach, but case studies support its effectiveness (Barry & Burlew, 2004) and it is often anecdotally reported to be useful.

Conclusions

Psychological approaches to the mental health and behavioural needs of children and young people with intellectual disabilities have much in common with those used with children and young people without intellectual disabilities who have mental health needs. Despite these commonalities, increased access to and efficacy of approaches requires specific modifications to established evidence-based interventions. Key modifications to approaches include continuing and increased emphasis on engagement and collaboration with the parents and families of children and young people with intellectual disabilities.

Although specific evaluations and evidence remains limited, the research available continues to support the use of behavioural and cognitive behavioural interventions. Prior to modified interventions being implemented, assessments of cognitive and emotional functioning will be required and this may include that of children and young people and their parents/carers. Such assessments will inform decision making in relation to the suitability of group and/or individual interventions and further inform intervention design. Where greater cognitive and functional impairment and severe behaviours that challenge may be present, there may be a justification for more extensively tailored and individualised approaches.

There also appears to be a significant overlap in relation to effective modified psychological approaches for children with intellectual disabilities, with and without autism spectrum conditions. Therefore, overall, it is suggested that there is a wide range of psychological approaches that, when modified appropriately, can be effective in supporting children and young people with intellectual disabilities and their families. However, their remains continuing needs for children and young people with intellectual disabilities and their families to be able to access appropriate multi-disciplinary and multi-agency support and interventions. These needs remain present in the context of limited resources within mental health services and across agencies.

Continuing to secure sufficient resources is needed in order to deliver effective interventions. Resources will also need to be identified for evaluating and researching modified approaches to ensure the continued development of evidence-based modified psychological interventions specifically for children and young people with intellectual disabilities.

References

Ball T, Bush A & Emerson E (2004) *Psychological Interventions for Severely Challenging Behaviours Shown by People with Intellectual disabilities.* Leicester: British Psychological Society.

Barry LM & Burlew SB (2004) Using Social Stories to teach choice and play skills to children with autism. *Focus on Autism and other Developmental Disabilities* (1) 45–51.

Beart S, Hardy G & Buchan L (2005) How people with intellectual disabilities view their social identity: a review of the literature. *Journal of Applied Research in Intellectual Disabilities* 47–56.

Beresford B (2009) The effectiveness of parent training interventions in improving problem behaviours among disabled children. *Research Works.* 2009–3. York: Social Policy Research Unit, University of York.

Carr EG, Levin L, McConnachie G, Carlson JI, Kemp DC & Smith CE (1994) *Communication-based Intervention for Problem Behaviour: A user's guide to producing positive change.* Baltimore: Brooks.

Dagnan D, Chadwick P & Proudlove J (2000) Towards an assessment of suitability of people with mental retardation for cognitive therapy. *Cognitive Therapy and Research* (6) 627–636.

Didden R, Duker PC & Korzilius H (1997) Meta-analytic study on treatment effectiveness for problem behaviours with individuals who have mental retardation. *American Journal of Mental Retardation* 387–399.

Eldevik S, Hastings RP, Hughes CJ, Jahrd E, Eikeseth S & Crosse S (2009) Meta-analysis of early intensive behavioural intervention for children with autism. *Journal of Clinical Child and Adolescent Psychology* (3) 439–450.

Emerson E (2001) *Challenging Behaviour.* Cambridge: Cambridge University Press.

Firth H & Rapley M (1990) *From Acquaintance to Friendship.* Kidderminster: BIMH Publications.

Fonagy P, Target M, Cotterell D, Phillips J & Kurtz Z (2002) *What Works for Whom? A critical review of treatments for children and adolescents.* New York: Guildford Press.

Gray C (1995) Teaching children with autism to "read" social situations. In: KA Qill (Ed) *Teaching Children with Autism: Strategies to enhance communication and socialization.* Albany, NY: Delmar.

Howlin P, Magiati I & Charman T (2009) Systematic review of early intensive behavioural interventions for children with autism. *American Journal on Intellectual and Developmental Disabilities* (1) 23–41.

Kavale KA & Forness SR (1996) Social skill deficits and intellectual disabilities: A meta-analysis. *Journal of Intellectual disabilities* (3) 226–237.

Kavale KA & Mostert MP (2004) Social skills interventions for individuals with intellectual disabilities. *Learning Disability Quarterly* (1) 31–43.

Lindsay WR, Nielson C & Lawrenson H (1997) Cognitive behaviour therapy for anxiety in people with intellectual disabilities. In: BS Kroese, D Dagnan & K Loumidis (Eds) *Cognitive-Behaviour Therapy for People with Intellectual disabilities*. Hove: Banner-Routledge.

Lovaas OI (1987) Behavioral treatment and normal educational and intellectual functioning in young autistic children. *Journal of Consulting and Clinical Psychology* 3–9.

McIntyre LL (2008) Adapting Webster-Stratton's incredible years parent training for children with developmental delay: finding from a treatment group only study. *Journal of Intellectual Disability Research* (12) 1176–1192.

Stallard P (2002) *Think Good, Feel Good*. Chichester: John Wiley & Sons.

Webster-Stratton C (2001) *The Incredible Years: Parent training* [online]. Available at: www.incredibleyears.com (accessed June 2020).

Williams-White S, Keonig K & Scahill L (2007) Social skills development in children with autism spectrum disorders: A review of the intervention research. *Journal of Autism and Developmental Disorders* 1858–1868.

Williams H & Jones RSP (1997) Teaching cognitive self-regulation of independence and emotion control skills. In: BS Kroese, D Dagnan & K Loumidis (Eds) *Cognitive-Behaviour Therapy for People with Intellectual disabilities*. Hove: Banner-Routledge.

Wilner P (2005) The effectiveness of psychotherapeutic interventions for people with intellectual disabilities: A critical review. *Journal of Intellectual Disability Research* (1) 73

Chapter 10: Psychopharmacological Approaches

Dr Alison Dunkerley

Chapter summary

This chapter reviews the use of psychopharmacological interventions for psychiatric disorder and behavioural difficulties presenting in children with intellectual disability. The prescribing of psychotropic drugs for this population remains a controversial issue, in part due to the small evidence base. The primary aim of this chapter is to summarise the current literature and guidelines relating to psychopharmacology in children and adolescents with intellectual disability, in order to provide practitioners with an understanding of the basic principles and the available psychopharmacological treatment options.

The chapter will cover pharmacological interventions for attention deficit hyperactivity disorder (ADHD); anxiety disorder; obsessive-compulsive disorder (OCD); depressive disorder; bipolar disorder; schizophrenia and other psychoses; aggression; self-injurious behaviour; sleep disorder; autism and tic disorder. It is not within the scope of this chapter to review all the medications used in clinical practice.

Background and common issues

The symptomatic presentation of psychiatric disorders in young people with intellectual disability (ID) may differ from those found in their typically developing peers. Clinicians often need to focus on observable behaviours such as aggression, levels of activity, sleep patterns and self-injurious behaviour. It is important in this population that we ensure that there is no diagnostic overshadowing; a term that describes blaming the condition/disability for the presentation, and can act as a barrier to the thorough, systematic evaluation of symptoms and signs that anyone without disabilities would expect.

The available data suggests that children with intellectual disability respond to various psychotropic medications in ways similar to their typically developing peers. However, rates of response tend to be poorer and the occurrence of side effects more frequent, with an increased vulnerability to potential drug-drug interactions (Calles, 2008). Monitoring the effects of medication closely is advised and continuation with treatment recommended only if clinical benefits can be demonstrated. Prescribing usually follows extrapolation from the evidence base that has been generated in the clinical trials.

Another problem is that many psychotropic medications are not licensed for use in children and adolescents, leading some clinicians to think that they cannot prescribe these. Licensing does not mean that a particular product is the only drug or member of a drug group to possess that particular action. Many drugs are relatively safe and potentially highly beneficial when used. The Medicines Act allows doctors to prescribe unlicensed medicines or to use licensed medicines for indications or in doses or by routes of administration outside the recommendations of the licence. It is important, however, to take care when documenting the decision-making process.

Communication problems can make it difficult for children to draw attention to early manifestations of side effects and hence suffer more severely from unwanted effects.

For patients with seriously impaired decisional autonomy and who are assessed as lacking capacity (Mental Capacity Act, 2005), who physically resist medications and clinically deteriorate as a result, concealed medication directed by an organisational policy of accountability is ethically justified. A management plan should be agreed following a best interests meeting.

At the time of writing this chapter, there is a three-year programme supported by NHS England – Stopping the over-medication of people with an intellectual disability, autism or both (STOMP), which was launched in 2016. STOMP-STAMP was launched in 2018. STAMP is an acronym for Supporting Treatment and Appropriate Medication in Paediatrics. Concern about the overuse of antipsychotic drugs has been a constant theme since the 1970s. However, despite a multitude of guidelines, the practice continues. The report into the events at Winterbourne View (an assessment unit for people with an intellectual disability, autism or both, who demonstrated challenging behaviours) not only raised concerns about the overuse of antipsychotic drugs but of antidepressants (South Gloucestershire Safeguarding Adults Board, 2012). Polypharmacy in people with ID is often driven by the introduction of multiple medicines intended to reduce the risk of future morbidity and mortality in specific health conditions e.g. epilepsy. Problematic polypharmacy may increase risk of drug interactions and adverse drug reactions. There is a need to optimise medicine use when there is polypharmacy to gain maximum benefit with least harm. Prescribers may not realise symptoms are iatrogenic and then prescribe even more drugs to counter the adverse effects of other drugs. A compromise is sometimes needed between the view of the prescriber and patient-informed choice (The Kings Fund, 2013). It is important to note that appropriate polypharmacy extends life expectancy and improves quality of life.

Young people with ID have a higher incidence of health difficulties. Some health problems may affect their swallowing. The problem of tablet swallowing may be overcome by simple adjustments e.g. changing the tablet from a circular to a torpedo shape. Chewing, crushing, or dispersing a tablet can cause a previously palatable tablet to become inedible or unpleasant. In addition to altering the taste, crushing, dispersing or chewing tablets/capsules before swallowing can affect how and where the drug is released into the body. Modified-release preparations should not be altered as the resultant dose release can increase the chance of side-effects and then leave a period of time when there is not enough in the body for it to be effective. The Human Medicines Regulations 2012 allow only independent prescribers to authorise unlicensed administration of medicines to patients; however, crushing, dispersing and mixing can be undertaken by a person acting under the written instructions of an independent prescriber. If tablets cannot be swallowed, an alternative liquid medicine or route of administration (patches, orodispersibles, suppositories) should be considered. Percutaneous endoscopic gastrostomy, also known as PEG, is where an external tube is inserted through a patient's abdominal wall and into their stomach. This is mainly used for feeding and nutritional support, although it can also be used for the administration of medication.

Attention Deficit Hyperactivity Disorder

Attention Deficit Hyperactivity Disorder (ADHD) is characterised by a persistent, developmentally inappropriate pattern of gross motor overactivity, inattention, and impulsivity that impairs educational, social and family functioning. ADHD responds to both behavioural and psychopharmacological treatments. Before changing medication, practitioners should consider the following:

- Have I titrated properly?
- Is the patient at the maximum dose?
- Is this drug/preparation working well at any times during the day?
- Have I got good enough information from school?
- Are parents and school in agreement about the effects of the drug?
- Am I targeting the right symptoms?
- Is there a behavioural explanation for the drug 'wearing off'?
- What else is going on in the patients' life/family life?

■ Is the medication working but the effects limited by side effects?

■ Have I missed any comorbidity?

■ Is the diagnosis right?

Stimulants

Where distractibility, poor concentration, restlessness, impulsivity and hyperactive behaviour is displayed in different settings (typically, at home, at school and in clinic), it is worth a trial of stimulant medication. A recent study (Simonoff *et al*, 2013) concluded that optimal dosing of methylphenidate is practical and effective in some children with hyperkinetic disorder and intellectual disability. Adverse effects typical of methylphenidate were seen and medication use may require close monitoring in this vulnerable group.

Stimulant medication results in a 70-80% favourable response in ADHD i.e. reduction in symptoms. The response occurs within 30 minutes of administration of the drug. Methylphenidate is the most common active ingredient in the majority of stimulant medications used. Long-duration preparations have been developed. Side-effects of short- and long-duration preparations include: abdominal pain, headaches, weight loss, reversible growth failure, anxiety, agitation, insomnia, increases in blood pressure and pulse rate, psychosis, tics and mood lability. Appetite suppression is sometimes a problem, so it may be preferable to give it after meals (although some preparations necessitate it to be given with food). Monitoring of appetite, weight, height, pulse rate and BP at least every six months is recommended.

In the case of weight/appetite loss, the use of high-calorific snacks and late evening meals should be encouraged. Possible further options include reducing the dose, switching to an alternative class of drugs or formulation, discontinuing medication on weekends or during the summer. Referral to a paediatric endocrinologist/growth specialist may be necessary if height and weight values are below critical thresholds.

Particularly severe adverse reactions to methylphenidate have been reported in velocardiofacial syndrome (Wang *et al*, 2000).

Best clinical practice should include a thorough assessment of all problematic symptoms before commencing a trial of stimulant medication to make identification and monitoring of drug side-effects easier. Seizure disorders should be well-controlled, and contraindicated conditions (e.g. psychosis) should be excluded before methylphenidate is started. There is emerging evidence that stimulant medication for ADHD does not increase seizure risk (Brikell *et al*, 2019).

The medical history should include enquiry about family history of heart disease, history of syncope with exercise and family history of sudden unexpected death <40 years.

Heart rate and blood pressure (with an age-adapted cuff) at rest should be obtained (repeated twice if HR > 100 beats/min, or BP > 95 percentile) at baseline and repeated every three to six months. If there is a resting heart rate > 110 or a history suggestive of arrhythmia or familial risk, then a 24-hour ECG should be obtained.

There is no evidence available for children with ADHD and congenital heart disease, however most children with cardiac problems, once stabilised by the paediatric cardiologists, may be treated with ADHD medications (Vetter *et al*, 2008). Initial titration of dosage to optimise response followed by regular predetermined appointments, at times suitable for child and parent attendance, and contact with the school is necessary. In order to improve adherence, it is worth setting meaningful and agreed targets with the child and their parents (e.g. improved modulation of behaviour, fewer negative interactions), reviewing side effects and utilising once-daily dosing with graded-release preparations. Long-term treatment and monitoring should be anticipated if the response is good. In the adolescent years attempts can be made to reduce or stop them at times of stability, but it is not necessary.

Some children benefit from dexamphetamine when methylphenidate has proved unsuccessful, or may respond without problems when methylphenidate has produced unacceptable adverse effects (e.g. mood lability). Lisdexamfetamine dimesylate (Elvanse), an orally-active dexamfetamine prodrug, is indicated for the treatment of attention-deficit hyperactivity disorder (ADHD) in children aged ≥ 6 years (including adolescents) when the response to methylphenidate (MPH) treatment is clinically inadequate. Lisdexamfetamine is generally well tolerated, with an adverse event profile (e.g. decreased appetite, headache, weight reduction, insomnia and irritability) typical of that reported for other stimulants. Thus, lisdexamfetamine provides an alternative option for the treatment of children and/ or adolescents with ADHD who have not responded adequately to previous ADHD pharmacotherapies.

Guanfacine

Guanfacine is an alpha 2 adrenergic agonist and hence a non-stimulant medication. In three short term, randomised controlled trials (RCTs) it was more effective than placebo at improving ADHD symptoms, although a beneficial effect on social functioning was not consistently shown. Guanfacine (Intuniv) is typically only used for ADHD when stimulants aren't suitable, not tolerated, or ineffective. It may take four to eight weeks to get the maximum benefit once the right dose is determined. However, improvements in some symptoms may occur sooner. Common side effects of guanfacine include: drowsiness, dizziness, dry mouth, constipation, tiredness, nausea, headache, stomach pain, weight gain or irritability. Serious adverse reactions include hypotension, weight increase, bradycardia and syncope. The tablet is usually taken once a day at bedtime. Guanfacine prolonged release was launched in the UK in February 2016.

Clonidine

Clonidine is an another α agonist (like guanfacine). A starting dose of 25 micrograms twice daily is recommended, increasing in 25 microgram increments up to a maximum of 150 micrograms twice daily. Before commencing clonidine, a careful cardiac history, examination and ECG should be undertaken. Resting BP and pulse needs to be monitored and if orthostatic changes are greater than 10%, consideration should be given to reducing the dosage.

Atomoxetine

Atomoxetine (Strattera) is a specific noradrenaline reuptake inhibitor which failed trials as an antidepressant. It was licensed in Europe in 2004 for ADHD. Side effects include nausea, vomiting, urinary hesitancy, rashes, weight loss, low mood and, rarely, suicidal thoughts/actions and, very rarely, hepatic failure. It has less potential for misuse and is used as an alternative to stimulant medication. It is more expensive than methylphenidate and is generally not used routinely as first line treatment except when there are clinically significant problems e.g. low weight, very poor appetite or sleep, tics, substance misuse or parents strongly against the use of stimulants.

Other treatment options

Historically, there has been an over-reliance on antipsychotic medication to control ADHD symptoms in this population. Low dose risperidone (i.e. commencing with 0.25mg once or twice daily) can be helpful (Aman *et al*, 2004).

Comorbid mental disorders are common and should be appropriately treated along with the treatment of the ADHD.

Anxiety disorders

Generally, anxiety disorders in children with intellectual disability do not require pharmacological intervention. Antidepressants, anxiolytics, antipsychotics, mood stabilizers, antiepileptic drugs and beta-blockers have been used to treat anxiety disorders in people with developmental disabilities.

Selective Serotonin Reuptake Inhibitors

The SSRIs are among the most commonly prescribed medications in young people with ASD (Hsia *et al*, 2014). Large randomised controlled medication trials for anxiety in young people with ASD are lacking, however. The data do highlight that young people with ASD may be particularly vulnerable to behavioural activation with certain SSRIs. Behavioural activation is a well-known side effect of SSRIs in children and is characterised by a cluster of symptoms including increased activity level, impulsivity, insomnia, or disinhibition without manic symptoms (Reinblatt *et al*, 2009). There is a small but significant increased relative risk for suicide on antidepressant versus placebo. To promote adherence with SSRI medication, spend time explaining to the family and child that most side-effects will usually resolve in the first several weeks. A baseline record of physical symptoms experienced by the child and adolescent can help to distinguish side-effects of medication from anxiety symptoms.

Social anxiety is part of the behavioural phenotype of fragile X and available studies suggest that SSRIs can be useful for managing anxiety and behavioural/emotional symptoms in individuals with fragile X (Calles, 2008). Drug treatment with SSRIs may also alleviate symptoms of severe anxiety in untreated PKU and Prader-Willi syndrome (Harris, 1998).

Obsessive-compulsive disorder

There are a number of clinical trials that indicate that clomipramine and other drugs which potently inhibit serotonin reuptake (the SSRIs) have therapeutic benefit in obsessive-compulsive disorder (OCD) presenting in children. A study administered cognitive-behavioural therapy (CBT), sertraline, and the combination to children and adolescents with OCD (The Paediatric OCD Treatment Study, 2003). Combining CBT and sertraline had the best outcome.

Selective Serotonin Reuptake Inhibitors

Sertraline has been granted a product licence for use in children and adolescents with OCD. There are reports describing the use of SSRIs in children with intellectual disability suffering from OCD and pervasive developmental disorders (PDD) with positive findings described e.g. decreased rate of rituals (Hollander *et al*, 2005).

Recent population studies support the association of OCD with post-streptococcal infection (Roupret & Kochman, 2002). Children with abrupt onset OCD should have a throat culture and if positive they should have antibiotic treatment.

Depressive disorder

Antidepressant medication can be beneficial in conjunction with individual and family work.

Where antidepressant medication is to be used, SSRIs are effective and justified as they have a more desirable side-effect profile than other antidepressants such as the tricyclics and monoamine oxidase inhibitors. This is important in young people with intellectual disabilities, where problems with concentration, continence or co-ordination of movement cause particular difficulties. After successful resolution of the acute symptoms, SSRIs should be continued for six months after remission (Depression in Children and Young People: identification and management, NICE, 2019). Some individuals require longer treatment. Fluoxetine has the best evidence base and should be used first-line in the treatment of depressive disorder in children and adolescents

Bipolar disorder

Most of the evidence on drug treatment for bipolar disorder comes from typically developing children and adults with intellectual disabilities. Antiepileptic drugs (used for their mood-stabilising effect) may be used as an alternative to lithium (Danielyan & Kowatch, 2005,) and is often preferred, given the high rate of seizure disorders (and nonparoxysmal EEG activity) in this population. Sodium valproate and lamotrigine are probably used most successfully for cyclical mood disorders. Sodium Valproate should not be offered to girls or young women of childbearing potential due to teratogenicity. If a decision is made to prescribe Valproate then the Pregnancy Prevention Programme must be followed[1]. Medication trials should continue for an adequate period of time. It is good practice to measure weight/BMI and take blood tests, if possible, for full blood count and liver function tests before starting sodium valproate and every six months thereafter. Blood testing is not an absolute requirement as it is with lithium.

Lithium is far from being a benign drug. Check electrolytes, creatinine, thyroid function tests, full blood count and urine specific gravity before commencing lithium. It requires diligent monitoring of the patient for neurotoxic side effects that may necessitate discontinuing lithium, including seizures, severe tremor, vomiting, lethargy and coma. Unwanted side effects that do not necessarily require stopping medication include polyuria with incontinence, gastrointestinal disturbance, hypothyroidism and dermatitis. It should be remembered that children who cannot tolerate needle sticks may require alternative medication.

Second-generation antipsychotics with combined dopaminergic and serotonergic properties also provide mood stabilisation. Aripiprazole is recommended as an

---

1   https://www.gov.uk/drug-safety-update/valproate-medicines-epilim-depakote-pregnancy-prevention-programme-materials-online

option for treating moderate to severe manic episodes in adolescents with bipolar I disorder, within its marketing authorisation (that is, up to 12 weeks of treatment for moderate to severe manic episodes in bipolar I disorder in adolescents aged 13 and older) (NICE TA 292, July 2013).

The combined treatments of a mood stabiliser (lithium or sodium valproate) and an antipsychotic may hold promise for long-term remission of symptoms (Hamrin & Pachler, 2007) in refractory cases.

Medication choice relies on many factors including child and family preference, presence of psychosis and side-effects.

Schizophrenia and other childhood psychoses

Onset of schizophrenia may occur in early adolescence and good therapeutic responses to antipsychotic medication have been evidenced at this age (Sikich et al, 2004). Later deterioration may be exacerbated if the condition is left untreated, whereas normal development may be re-established if effective treatment is given.

A Cochrane review (Kennedy, 2007) for childhood-onset schizophrenia found no superiority of second-generation antipsychotics (SGAs) over first-generation antipsychotics (FGAs) such as haloperidol.

The use of antipsychotic drugs is associated with significant risks of extra pyramidal symptoms (EPS) and tardive dyskinesia (TD), particularly the FGAs. Other side-effects include weight gain, sedation and prolactin level increase (see Table 10.1). Metabolic complications are associated with the SGAs such as risperidone and olanzapine. Bobo et al (2013) indicated that children and adolescents prescribed antipsychotics had a threefold increased risk for type II diabetes.

Table 10:1: Side-effects of antipsychotic drugs (indicating likelihood of producing the side-effect)

Weight gain (development of metabolic syndrome)	Prolactin level increase	Sedation	EPSE
Clozapine Olanzapine Risperidone Quetiapine Amisulpiride Aripiprazole ↑	Risperidone Amisulpiride Haloperidol Olanzapine Quetiapine Clozapine Aripiprazole ↑	Quetiapine Clozapine Olanzapine Risperidone Amisulpiride Haloperidol ↑	Haloperidol Amisulpiride Risperidone Olanzapine Quetiapine Clozapine ↑

Hyperprolactinaemia can result in several side-effects such as: amenorrhoea and oligomenorrhoea, erectile dysfunction, hirsutism and galactorrhoea. The effect of increased prolactin levels on growth (including bone mineral density) and sexual maturation is not known (Morgan & Taylor, 2007). Children and adolescents may be at greater risk for certain side effects (e.g. enuresis) than adults (Aman *et al*, 2005). Weight gain is greater in children and adolescents than in adults (Correll, 2006) and they appear more sensitive than adults to extra pyramidal side-effects (Correll, 2008).

Fluoxetine may increase the blood levels and effects of Aripiprazole. This can increase the likelihood of developing side effects such as drowsiness, seizure, Parkinson-like symptoms, abnormal muscle movements and low blood pressure.

The possible increased risk of adverse side-effects necessitates ongoing review in order to ensure the fewest number of drugs are used at the lowest possible dose that will satisfactorily control symptoms. Using higher than the recommended British National Formulary doses of antipsychotics does not appear to increase efficacy (Council Report CR138, Royal College of Psychiatrists, 2005).

Monitoring use of medication

Practitioners should monitor young patients at baseline and at regular three to six monthly intervals for height, weight, possible sexual side effects, behavioural change, extra pyramidal symptoms, bowel habit, blood pressure and pulse. Blood testing can be difficult but, if a child is more than 10 centile points above the expected weight, fasting blood glucose and lipid concentrations should be measured following a risk-benefit analysis with carers. This will help prevent medical illness associated with excessive weight, such as type 2 diabetes. Urinary glucose testing may be done if a blood test is not possible. It is not clear how frequently metabolic syndrome of – dyslipidaemia, glucose intolerance, hypertension and abdominal obesity – occurs in children and adolescents but hyperlipidaemia is common in Smith-Magenis syndrome and, therefore, SGAs are best avoided in this condition.

A history of epilepsy should always be sought as this condition affects approximately a third of children with moderate to profound intellectual disability and antipsychotic medications are known to lower the seizure threshold, especially clozapine. Liaison with the treating paediatrician or neurologist is recommended, who may consider titrating the dose of anti-epileptic medication if the seizure burden increases.

Clozapine can be used in refractory cases of schizophrenia (Gogtay, 2008) but requires careful blood count monitoring for possible bone marrow suppression.

The risks that go with using these drugs must be balanced against the unquestionable benefits from treatment for the vast majority of people when used appropriately (Kumra, 2008).

Anticholinergic drugs to treat the movement disorders side-effects arising from the use of antipsychotic drugs should be considered in the following circumstances: prescribing of high doses; a previous history of extra-pyramidal reactions; and when unwanted effects are not adequately controlled despite decreasing the dosage of antipsychotic medication. They have no effect on akathisia, they may have an effect on mood and they can precipitate an episode of intestinal obstruction in people with intellectual disability who suffer from severe constipation.

Challenging behaviour and intellectual disability

Aggression

Drug treatment of aggression is a problematic and often disputed issue. Positive Behaviour Support (PBS) is currently considered to be the best practice approach to supporting individuals with intellectual disabilities who present with complex and challenging behaviour. PBS provides a person-centred and values-based, multi-component framework for assessing and understanding challenging behaviour using functional assessment. This leads to a formulation-based support plan that can draw upon a broad range of theoretically informed interventions, focusing on developing the quality of life of individuals and reducing levels of challenging behaviour and the use of restrictive practice (BPS, 2018).

NICE guidelines now exist for using psychotropic medicines in people with intellectual disability whose behaviour challenges. The guidance was updated in March 2019. There is evidence of widespread prescribing of psychotropic medicines (antipsychotics, antidepressants and hypnotics) for people with intellectual disabilities, many of whom do not have relevant indications recorded for the psychotropic medicines they are prescribed. Antipsychotic medication should only be considered to manage behaviour that challenges in people with intellectual disabilities when other interventions have not been helpful and when the risk to the person or others is very severe. They should only be offered in combination with psychological or other interventions to help manage challenging behaviour. Local policies relating to the treatment of challenging behaviour in people with intellectual disabilities should be reviewed to ensure these are in line with the NICE guideline on challenging behaviour and learning disabilities[2].

---

2   See www.nice.org.uk/guidance/ng11

Within the last 10 years, an increase in clinical research has attempted to provide efficacy and safety data to support the use of medications in children with Pervasive Developmental Disorders associated with aggression and irritability. Of the SGAs, risperidone has the largest amount of evidence. Well-conducted, double-blind placebo controlled studies have shown that risperidone significantly improves behavioural problems including aggression (McCracken *et al*, 2002; Shea *et al*, 2004). Dosing should be initiated at 0.25 mg per day for patients < 20 kg and 0.5 mg per day for patients ≥ 20 kg. After a minimum of four days from treatment initiation, the dose may be increased to the recommended dose of 0.5 mg per day for patients < 20 kg and 1 mg per day for patients ≥ 20 kg. The maximum daily dose of risperidone in one of the pivotal trials, when the therapeutic effect reached plateau, was 1 mg in patients < 20 kg, 2.5 mg in patients ≥ 20 kg, or 3 mg in patients > 45 kg. A Cochrane review (Jesner, 2007) showed some evidence of the benefits of risperidone in treating irritability, repetitive behaviours and social withdrawal in ASD. The authors stressed, however, that the findings from the review should be treated with caution as small sample sizes and the lack of a standardised outcome measure preclude the making of meaningful inferences.

Safety analyses of studies indicated that low-dose risperidone appears to be associated with a low risk of movement disorders, prolactin-related adverse events, and cognitive decline. However, concerns have been highlighted over metabolic side-effects (Malone & Waheed, 2009). Weight gain from risperidone has led to the use of aripiprazole (Valicenti-McDermott & Demb, 2006). Aripiprazole is efficacious, generally safe and well tolerated in the treatment of children and adolescents with aggression associated with developmental disabilities (Stigler, 2009).

Recording problematic behaviours (intensity and frequency) for a set period before prescribing is desirable. A clear understanding of the reasons behind the prescribing of psychotropic medication and its appropriate use in the management of aggressive behaviour is necessary. Informed consent from carers for the use of medication is advisable. In this complex area of clinical practice, the use of drugs should be carefully monitored to determine whether medication can be withdrawn without negative effects on behaviour and any symptomatic benefit balanced against side-effects that may occur. The same monitoring and testing procedures for antipsychotic medication, described in the section on schizophrenia, should be undertaken. Prescribing antipsychotic medication in the very young (under five years of age) is generally not recommended.

Carbamazepine has been used to treat aggressive behaviours, especially when EEG abnormalities or high rates of seizure activity are present. When carbamazepine is added to aripiprazole, the aripiprazole dose should be doubled. Additional dose increases should be based on clinical evaluation. If carbamazepine is later withdrawn, the aripiprazole dose should be reduced. Sodium valproate has also been reported to be of benefit for people with developmental disability and associated aggressive behaviour (Ruedrich *et al*, 1999), as has topiramate (Harden *et al*, 2004). Quick-acting benzodiazepine drugs can be used to treat acute aggressive episodes, but beware of habituation, tolerance and addiction in the medium to long term. Lorazepam and midazolam administered by the buccal route are preferred because of their relatively short half-lives. An increase in aggression can occasionally occur and alternative interventions should be attempted.

Self-injurious behaviour

There are a number of factors predisposing to, precipitating and maintaining self-injury in young people with intellectual disability. Psychopharmacological approaches should be considered only where environmental modification and behavioural interventions have failed to reduce levels of self-injurious behaviour (SIB). Adequate treatment of co-morbid conditions is necessary.

The extreme distress of severe self-injurious behaviour with significant effect on quality of life despite environmental and cognitive-behavioural interventions results in frequent requests for the use of medication by carers. Between 30%-50% of individuals with SIB are reported to receive psychotropic drugs. Treatment targets should be realistic, especially when dealing with persistent or entrenched behaviour. Case studies predominate as the evidence for psychopharmacological approaches, rarely double-blind placebo-controlled trials.

Historically, antipsychotic drugs have been the most widely used form of medication in the management of SIB (Verhoeven & Tuinier, 2001). Risperidone has been shown to be effective and well tolerated for the treatment of SIB in children with autistic disorder (McCracken *et al*, 2002). One study showed that although frequency of SIB is reduced, duration and severity may not be significantly altered (Canitano, 2006). Risperidone can also be tried in cri-du-chat syndrome as the stereotypical behaviours (e.g. body rocking, hand waving) can respond to dopaminergic blockade and may share an aetiological connection with self-injurious behaviour seen in other children. Aripiprazole is also safe and well-tolerated (Marcus, 2009).

SSRIs can be used, especially if self-injurious behaviour appears to be associated with depressive features, anxiety or obsessive-compulsive features. A beneficial effect from fluoxetine on the skin-picking and overeating associated with Prader-Willi syndrome has been evidenced (Soni, 2007).

Naltrexone, an opiate antagonist, is used in this area of clinical practice. Start with 0.5mg/kg/day, increasing slowly to a maximum dose of 2mg/kg/day. The use of naltrexone is based on the hypothesis that self-injury causes the release of naturally occurring opioids which raise the pain threshold, hence reducing the disagreeable emotional features of suffering associated with self-injurious behaviour. Naltrexone may be less effective for children because the effects of opiates differ in the brain at different stages of development. Also, reports on the effectiveness of naltrexone in the treatment of SIB have not supported the use of this drug (Symons *et al*, 2004).

Sleep disorders

Sleep disorders are common in children with intellectual disability. The establishment of normal sleep patterns can have dramatic beneficial effects on functioning and behaviour for children. Medical causes e.g. obstructive sleep apnoea due to hypotonia, obesity, ENT problems and anatomical abnormalities, should be excluded. Nocturnal seizures should also be considered.

Sleep hygiene measures, bedtime routines, modification of social and environmental factors, and psychological therapies should be used primarily with those suffering with sleep disorders. Ensure potential stimulants (caffeine, food colourings and flavourings, excessive TV watching or computer use) are minimised. These interventions are, however, insufficient in many children and concomitant drug therapy can be valuable.

Melatonin is a useful medication to promote sleep. Melatonin is a hormone secreted by the pineal gland. It has been shown to have a central role in sleep initiation. During the past decade, more studies and case reports have provided encouraging results in paediatric patient groups (Giannotti *et al*, 2006; Garstang *et al*, 2006). The MENDS study (2012, Gringas) compared IR melatonin v placebo in children with neurodevelopmental disorder and found significant improvement in initiation of sleep. Beta-blocker drugs, such as atenolol and propranolol, are a class of drugs that seem to lower melatonin levels. This might cause problems sleeping. Research suggests that taking a melatonin supplement might reduce this side effect. Treatment with melatoninergic agonists seems to be promising in another disorder, Smith-Magenis syndrome, in which the melatonin rhythm is mainly reversed (Fabiano & Leersnyder, 2007). In this congenital disorder, a sustained high nocturnal level of melatonin would be important, therefore the use of a prolonged-release formulation would be indicated.

In most children, melatonin is given 30 minutes before the desired bedtime. It is sensible to start with a low dose, for example 2 to 3mg in infants and toddlers and increase in 0.5 to 3mg increments, depending on effect, going up to 8mg. In some children, the sleep difficulties disappear after the first dose, in others the improvement takes days or weeks and sometimes there is no desired effect. The duration of treatment is variable. It is important to ensure a synthetic preparation is used, rather than one derived from human or animal tissue, because there is a theoretical risk of slow virus transmission. Significant side effects are not recorded. There is often habituation but this does not affect everyone.

Promethazine (Phenergan) is an antihistamine sometimes used as a sleeping pill.

Clonidine may be beneficial for repeated night-time waking, including insomnia aggravated by stimulant medication. In Williams syndrome there are excessive periodic limb movements during sleep and benzodiazepines, e.g. clonazepam, are indicated.

Tourette's syndrome/Tics

Tourette's syndrome is not as rare as it was once believed to be. Comprehensive behavioural intervention including multiple strategies can reduce impairment significantly (Woods *et al*, 2009). Possible indications for drug treatment include interference with daily functioning, pain and/or injury, social problems or impact on learning.

If tic suppressing drugs are needed, a two-tier approach and monotherapy constitute the best practice. First tier drugs, notably α adrenergic agonists, are recommended for people with both tics and attention-deficit/hyperactivity disorder. Treatment with clonidine begins with 0.025 to 0.05mg/day and is increased in increments of 0.025 to 0.05mg/day every five to seven days. Adverse effects of clonidine include sedation, cognitive blunting, irritability, headaches, decreased salivation and, at higher doses, hypotension and dizziness (monitor as in section on ADHD, page 131). Guanfacine can also be considered, particularly if there is comorbid ADHD. Second tier drugs include various typical and atypical neuroleptics. Use the lowest possible dose (1.0-2.5mg/day) at bedtime (two divided doses may give better control through the day).

However, few studies have compared the short term or long term efficacy and safety of different psychopharmacological agents, so no drug has been proved to be superior. New agents are needed given the limited benefit and potential side effects, such as weight gain (see section on schizophrenia on page 137 for side effect profiles) associated with the use of some neuroleptics.

Higher doses of antipsychotics and clonidine are not necessarily more effective but are more frequently associated with sedation. Reducing dosage can be beneficial where higher doses have failed. Paradoxically, one study found that in children with autism and intellectual disability tics can appear with risperidone therapy (Feroz-Nainar & Roy, 2006). The use of multiple drugs in combination with risperidone increased the likelihood of tics occurring, and at a lower dosage, compared to monotherapy

Methylphenidate and clonidine (particularly in combination) are effective for ADHD in children with co-morbid tics (Tourette Syndrome Study Group, 2002). However, it should be noted that serious adverse effects have been reported with concomitant use of methylphenidate and clonidine, although a causal relationship has not been established and the safety of using a combination of methylphenidate and clonidine has not been evaluated systematically (RCPsych).

Autism Spectrum Disorder (ASD)

At the present time there is no medication to treat autism. It is important to recognise and diagnose comorbid conditions.

At the time of writing there is an international, multi-site trial occurring that aims to test if bumetanide can improve some of the core symptoms of autism and also to test its safety.

In people with ASD it is thought there is a difference in how neurons have developed and process information. One theory is that the level of 'chloride' in the neurons is too high and this affects how the neurons are stimulated and build connections. Bumetanide (a well-known drug) is being tested because it reduces chloride levels in the kidney but it also acts in the brain. A trial testing bumetanide in 88 children has shown interesting results. Significant improvements in different aspects of autism were shown in children who received bumetanide and completed the trial.

Key learning points

- The aims of psychopharmacological interventions should be regularly reviewed.
- Medication used in clinical practice must have proven safety for the individual child/young person.
- Decisions should be evidence-based, where possible.
- Clinicians practising in this area should be well-versed in the most current and slowly growing research on psychotropic medication.
- Inadequacies in care provision must not be masked by the indiscriminate use of symptom-controlling drugs.
- Children/young people with intellectual disability should not be denied effective treatment with medication for the treatment of their mental health problems.

References

Aman MG, Arnold LE, Lindsay R, Nash P *et al* (2005) Risperidone treatment of autistic disorder: longer-term benefits and blinded discontinuation after 6 months. *American Journal of Psychiatry* **162** (7) 1361–1369.

Berry-Kravis E & Potanos K (2004) Psychopharmacology in fragile X syndrome--present and future. *Mental Retardation & Developmental Disabilities Research Reviews* **10** (1) 42–8.

Bobo WV, Cooper WO, Stein CM et al (2013) Antipsychotics and the risk of type 2 diabetes mellitus in children and youth. *JAMA Psychiatry* **70** 1067–75.

Brikell I, Chen Q, Kuja-Halkola R, D'Onofrio B *et al* (2019) Medication treatment for attention-deficit/ hyperactivity disorder and the risk of acute seizures in individuals with epilepsy. *Epilepsia* **60** (2) 284–293.

Brylewski J & Duggan L (2008) Antipsychotic Medication for Challenging Behaviour in People with Learning Disability. *The Cochrane Collaboration*, Wiley.

Calles JL (2008) Use of Psychotropic Medications in Children with Developmental Disabilities. *Paediatric Clinics of North America*, **55**(5),1227-1240.

Chaplin S (2016) Guanfacine to control ADHD in children and adolescents. *Prescriber* **27** (7) 37–38.

Danielyan A & Kowatch RA (2005) Management options for bipolar disorder in children and adolescents. *Paediatric Drugs* **7** 277–294.

Duerdan M, Avery T & Payne R (2013) Polypharmacy and Medicines Optimisation. Kings Fund.

Dunkerley A (2009) Medical. In: Bernard S & Turk J (Eds) *Developing Mental Health Services for Children and Adolescents with Learning Disabilities: A Toolkit for Clinicians*. RCPsych Publications.

Elchaar GM, Maisch NM, Gianni Augusto LM & Wehring HJ (2006) Efficacy and safety of naltrexone use in paediatric patients with autistic disorder. *Annals of Pharmacotherapy*, **40** (6) 1086–1095.

Greenaway M & Elbe D (2009) Focus on Aripiprazole: A Review of its use in Child and Adolescent Psychiatry. *Journal of the Canadian Acadamy of Child and Adolescent Psychiatry*, **18** (3) 250–260.

Greydanus D, Calles J & Patel D (2008) *Pediatric and Adolescent Psychopharmacology*. Cambridge University Press.

Hsia Y, Wong AY, Murphy DG, Simonoff E, Buitelaar JK & Wong IC (2014) Psychopharmacological prescriptions for people with autism spectrum disorder (ASD): A multinational study. *Psychopharmacology* **231** (6) 999–1009.

Hadjikhani N, Zürcher NR, Rogier O, Ruest T, Hippolyte L, Ben-Ari Y & Lemonnier E (2015) Improving emotional face perception in autism with diuretic bumetanide: A proof-of-concept behavioral and functional brain imaging pilot study. *Autism* **19** (2) 149–157.

Handen BL & Gilchrist R (2006) Practitioner review: Psychopharmacology in children and adolescents with mental retardation. *Journal of Child Psychology and Psychiatry and Allied Disciplines* **47** (9) 871–882.

Ingrassia A & Turk J (2005) The use of clonidine for severe and intractable sleep problems in children with neurodevelopmental disorders: a case series. *European Child & Adolescent Psychiatry* **14** 34–40.

Jesner OS, Aref-Adib M & Coren E (2007) Risperidone for autism spectrum disorder. Cochrane Database of Systematic *Reviews* 1: CD005040

Marcus RN, Owen R, Kamen L *et al* (2009) A placebo-controlled, fixed-dose study of aripiprazole in children and adolescents with irritability associated with autistic disorder. *Journal of the American Academy of Child and Adolescent Psychiatry* **48** 1110–9.

NICE guideline [NG11] (2015) *Challenging behaviour and learning disabilities: prevention and interventions for people with learning disabilities whose behaviour challenges* [online]. Available at: www. nice.org.uk/guidance/ng11 (accessed June 2020).

NICE guideline [NG87] (2018) *Attention Deficit Hyperactivity Disorder: Diagnosis and Management* [online]. Available at: www.nice.org.uk/guidance/ng87 (accessed June 2020).

NICE guideline [NG134] (2019) *Depression in children and young people: identification and management* [online]. Available at: www.nice.org.uk/guidance/ng134 (accessed June 2020).

Pearson DA, Lane DM, Santos CW *et al* (2004) Effects of methylphenidate treatment in children with mental retardation and ADHD: individual variation in medication response. *Journal of the American Academy of Child & Adolescent Psychiatry* **43** 686–698.

Pearson DA, Santos CW, Casat CD *et al* (2004a) Treatment effects of methylphenidate on cognitive functioning in children with mental retardation and ADHD. *Journal of the American Academy of Child & Adolescent Psychiatry* **43** 677–685.

Pearson DA, Santos CW, Roache JD *et al* (2003) Treatment effects of methylphenidate on behavioral adjustment in children with mental retardation and ADHD. *Journal of the American Academy of Child & Adolescent Psychiatry* **42** 209–216.

Reinblatt SP, DosReis S, Walkup JT & Riddle MA (2009) Activation adverse events induced by the selective serotonin reuptake inhibitor fluvoxamine in children and adolescents. *Journal of Child and Adolescent Psychopharmacology* **19** (2) 119–126.

Santosh PJ & Singh J (2016) Drug treatment of autism spectrum disorder and its comorbidities in children and adolescents. *Advances in Psychiatric Treatment* **22** 151–161.

Simonoff E, Taylor E, Baird G, Bernard S, Chadwick O, Liang H & Jichi F (2013) Randomized controlled double-blind trial of optimal dose methylphenidate in children and adolescents with severe attention deficit hyperactivity disorder and intellectual disability. *Journal of Child Psychology and Psychiatry* **54** 527–535.

Turk J (2003) Melatonin supplementation for severe and intractable sleep disturbance in young people with developmental disabilities: short review and commentary. *Journal of Medical Genetics* **40** 793–796.

Turk J (2007) Intellectual (Learning) Disability and Drug Therapy. In: Turk J, Graham P & Verhulst F (Eds) *Child & Adolescent Psychiatry, a Developmental Approach*. Oxford: Oxford University Press.

Vetter VL, Elia J, Erickson C *et al* (2009) Cardiovascular monitoring of children and adolescents with heart disease receiving medications for attention deficit/hyperactivity disorder [corrected]: a scientific statement from the American Heart Association Council on Cardiovascular Disease in the Young Congenital Cardiac Defects Committee and the Council on Cardiovascular Nursing. *American Heart Association Council on Cardiovascular Disease in the Young Congenital Cardiac Defects Committee; American Heart Association Council on Cardiovascular Nursing.*

Chapter 11: Mental Health Service Provision

Dr Mark Lovell and Martha Laxton-Kane

Chapter summary

This chapter covers the provision of services for children and young people with moderate to profound intellectual disabilities. England will be used as a basis for the descriptions of service models and the socio-political context within which these have been developed. Staff composition, skill set and what a service should be offering irrespective of service model design is described. An overview is provided based upon the experience and views of the authors working in different service models, in different parts of England with differing professional backgrounds.

Introduction

In recent years there has been an increased awareness and emphasis on the needs (and unmet needs) of children and young people (CYP) with intellectual disabilities (ID). Using England as an example, there have been a number of key areas that merit discussion.

Transforming Care (Department of Health, 2012) has emphasised the need to manage CYP with ID and autism (and adults) in the community rather than in inpatient settings, with the transfer of financial resources to intensive home treatment teams and a reduction in the number of national CYP ID beds. As part of transforming care, there has been a programme named 'new care models', which though not directly affecting CYP with moderate to profound ID, has resulted in the integration of CYP with mild ID into 'generic' CYP mental health inpatient units, thus altering the patient mix in the ID inpatient units.

The STOMP-STAMP campaign (STopping Over-Medication of People with learning disability, autism or both, and Supporting Treatment and Appropriate Medication in Paediatrics) has emphasised the historical practice of over or inappropriate prescribing and poor practice in the assessment, prescribing and monitoring of psychoactive medications for mental health and behavioural conditions, which sometimes leads to harm or unnecessary treatment (NHS England, 2019).

The National Institute for Health and Care Excellence (www.NICE.org) has numerous guidance documents that advise on the care of CYP with ID with summaries of the available research and recommendations for gold standard evidence based or expert recommended care. These include topics such as Attention Deficit Hyperactivity Disorder (ADHD), ASD diagnosis and management, challenging behaviour assessment, management and services, as well as numerous mental health topics of relevance such as anxiety.

Positive Behaviour Support (PBS) has gained traction as an ethical approach to assessing, understanding and managing behaviour that challenges others. It is a variant of Applied Behavioural Analysis (ABA) that only uses positive approaches, signifying a move away from sanction-based and aversive systems to manage behaviours. This was driven by investigations into the abusive management of people with ID and/or autism at Winterbourne View (Department of Health, 2012) and has led to the creation of a PBS framework (Positive Behaviour Support Academy, 2015).

High profile influences have arisen through the reports by Sir Martin Narey (Narey, 2016) and Dame Christine Lenehan (Lenehan, 2017a; 2017b). Specific groups of clinicians have been tasked with considering their roles and responsibilities, and challenges have been made to the wider health, education and care system to improve care for children and young people with ID and/or autism with mental health problems or challenging behaviour.

In summary, there has been an increased national focus (in England) in response to the unmet needs of CYP with ID in particular with regards to their mental health, behaviours that challenge others, location of care, medications and service provision to meet their needs. These, along with guidance, will hopefully drive up both the quantity and quality of services offered.

Service models

To meet the mental health and behaviour needs of CYP with ID there are a variety of models currently in place. Each of these will be covered, considering the relative merits and potential disadvantages of each. This list is not exhaustive and there may be models incorporating different components.

Table 11.1: Community models

Service Description	Advantages	Disadvantages
ID-CAMHS including mild ID	Adult services usually include mild ID and service structure can be similar for CYP with ID in what is offered and by whom. Also, other services e.g. special schools and disability social care in some geographical areas, are more likely to be seeing the same CYP.	Many CYP with mild ID have mental health/behaviour needs more akin to those of CYP without an ID. Capacity/ability to self-engage/disengage with services are more likely. Requires a wider skill set needed by staff.
ID-CAMHS alongside CAMHS/joint service with 2 distinct teams	This model creates a model of parity of esteem between non-ID and ID-CAMHS and allows the 2 services to work in parallel, jointly, or to provide differing services and make reasonable adjustments to meet the differing needs of the CYP they cater for. Service provision can overlap to meet the primary needs of the child and increase skill sets and shared roles.	The main disadvantage of this model is that CYP can fall between the gaps or have a potential transition point between CAMHS and ID-CAMHS if an ID is identified or an ID diagnosis is removed. Services may lack flexibility in who is seen thus preventing cross over of skills/knowledge to meet a CYP's needs irrespective of diagnostic status.
CAMHS incorporating ID, no separate service (for mental health and/or behaviour)	There are no gaps in service between CAMHS and ID-CAMHS, an equal/equitable service and the ability to meet the wider needs of CYP with mental health or behaviours irrespective of ability. This model promotes the concept that the individual is a child or young person first and not a diagnosis or level of ability. Simpler for the referrer.	Unless there are specialist sub-teams or workers with additional knowledge, skills and differing employment arrangements to adjust for the disability (e.g. more community/school based, flexibility in approach, longer term input etc), then skills may be either diluted within staff or reasonable adjustments are not made offering a one-size-fits-all approach. Mental disorders may be diagnostically overshadowed by the ID and missed. Distress and behaviours related to a variety of functions may be dismissed as →

Service Description	Advantages	Disadvantages
CAMHS incorporating ID, no separate service (for mental health and/or behaviour) Continued		'behavioural' and not meeting criteria for service (if behaviour is not included). Service pressures for meeting the needs of CYP in crisis e.g. deliberate self-harm and severe mental illness may reduce the available service offer for CYP with ID, thus not offering an equal/ equitable service.
ID-CAMHS with CAMHS and Paediatrics	This model emphasises a holistic child-based health approach first, allowing bio-psycho-social approaches. Often for CYP with ID, physical and mental health are linked and hard to separate or may present in the same ways. Overlapping skills can be utilised and there is a collective responsibility for a CYP's health. Communication between health professionals is improved and easier and cross referrals are simpler.	It is likely to be within an acute hospital (physical health) setting without other mental health services. Establishing parity of esteem for mental health may prove difficult as a single specialty within a wider context and physical health priorities/targets/budgets may dominate financial and service discussions.
ID-CAMHS in the same hospital/trust as all other Mental Health Services	All the services available have a focus on mental health and/or behaviour. There will be clear cross service overlaps and all mental health transitions will be within the same over-arching hospital/trust. This can maintain professional relationships, add flexibility to transitions and allow shared record keeping through an individual's time in service.	There is limited access to joint physical care and co-working between physical and mental health/behavioural services, so less co-working between YP pathways of care which YP with ID more likely have many health professionals involved. This model emphasises mental health, diagnosis of ID or behaviour need first, over age. Transitions still occur at aged 18 to another team. →

Service Description	Advantages	Disadvantages
ID-CAMHS co-located with Social Care	This has clear advantages in terms of communication and joint working to meet a CYP's needs from a psycho-social perspective.	Unless the services are co-funded, then there is a risk to either service should demands increase or priorities change e.g. safeguarding, out of area placement costs or complex health package costs increase. Location of CAMHS and paediatrics may influence interagency relationships/communication.
0-25 service	This model acknowledges that CYP with ID are often still developing into their early 20s and avoids a service transition point at adulthood when many other services are changing e.g. paediatric to adult health/GP, school to college, children's social care to adult social care etc. and mental health/behaviour may change as a consequence. This is in line with England Special Educational Needs provision (SEND).	Many clinical staff train to work either with CYP or adults and are not skilled or knowledgeable about the different models of care, or even qualified to work with the other group. This poses challenges for service design and management. Furthermore, many other services are aligned on a 0-18 model.
All age ID services	There is no transition between CYP and adult services offering continuity of care from childhood into adulthood.	The main disadvantage of this model is that children are not little adults, and conversely, adults are not big children. Staff need to be skilled and knowledgeable in the management of mental health and behaviours in both CYP and adults irrespective of background training. This maintains not just a neurodevelopmental perspective but also a developmental perspective and the ability to operate in both CYP and Adult multiagency arenas. With CYP, much therapeutic work is done within the context of the family. →

Service Description	Advantages	Disadvantages
No ID-CAMHS service	There are no advantages to this model. Commissioners may, however, see this model as cheaper (at face value).	This model is unfortunately the status quo in some areas. This does not meet the needs of CYP with ID, and in fact discriminates against them, not reasonably adjusting. A lack of CYP service may allow unmanaged/untreated mental health and behaviour conditions to worsen and then present at adult ID services. The CYP, their family and wider multiagency system may have suffered harm in the interim. This is likely to incur more costs and increase the use of inpatient services.
Positive Behaviour Services/ Challenging Behaviour Services	These services offer specific positive behaviour based assessments and treatment for CYP with ID and challenging behaviour. They are often able to offer more intensive focused specialised work for CYP with more severe behaviours. They often supplement ID-CAMHS/ CAMHS.	Staff in the non-specialist team may become de-skilled, or there are transitions between different parts of a service if behaviours are more severe. There is a risk of creating service boundaries, missing mental health presentations if staff are not skilled in this area and working in isolation.
Crisis teams	Crisis teams may function all day and all week or only at certain times out of hours. They are predominantly for crisis mental health presentations and are variable as to whether they manage behaviour crises in CYP with ID. If they have staff with experience of managing ID crises, they can be a helpful add-on to ID-CAMHS services.	For crisis teams that only manage mental health crises and not behaviours within the context of ID, they can be seen as unhelpful or miss the function of a behaviour, recognising only mental health as causality. This can increase the risk of mental health act assessment referrals, rather than adopting positive behaviour support approaches. There is a risk of the creation of service boundaries and working in isolation. →

Service Description	Advantages	Disadvantages
Intensive Home Treatment Teams (non ID or ID specific IHTT)	These are designed to reduce the need for hospital admission or to assist in the return to the community once admitted. Non-ID specific services can be helpful in assisting with keeping a CYP out of hospital, particularly if at the high end of the ID IQ spectrum and able to engage with therapeutic intervention. ID specific variants are being trialled at the time of writing.	Reasonable adjustments are often required to make these models work in ID e.g. shorter sessions, more frequent and repeated intervention over a longer period, with simpler language used and other adaptations to the needs of CYP with ID. Service commissioning may not allow for this. There is a risk of the creation of service boundaries, additional transitions and working in isolation.

Table 11.2: Inpatient/Residential Models

Service Description	Advantages	Disadvantages
Challenging behaviour assessment and treatment	There are some services that offer time-limited stays to focus on challenging behaviours with the intention of avoiding inpatient admissions or the need for residential care/education (Reid et al, 2013).	Though designed to be assessment and treatment for behaviour, they may miss mental health or physical health presentations if the skills of the clinical team are only behaviour-focused.
Tier 4/ open/ secure/ with/ without generic/ mild ID	Psychiatric inpatient services for CYP with ID are limited in their number. They are nationally commissioned (NHS England) or are private/charitable hospitals. There are units for younger CYP with ID or those with severe to profound ID, 'open' wards for adolescents or services at low/medium secure level. At times 'generic' units will take CYP with mild ID. They serve a purpose for assessing and treating CYP with ID and mental health or severe behaviour presentations. Their main advantage is an ability to assess and manage/treat a CYP over the 24-hour period in a safe and secure environment away from the home/school.	Distance from home is often the main disadvantage, since these are in the main regional/ national services. Also, improvements gained may not be transferable to the home setting owing to the resources required. They are also, not in keeping with the Transforming Care agenda of care in the community.

What is the preferred service model?

Each area of the UK has its own variant on the above options to meet the mental health and behaviour needs of CYP with ID. Each comes with its own advantages and disadvantages. They are generally a product of past commissioning decisions and local innovation and leadership. It is likely that the 'ideal' service does not exist and would probably be an ID-CAMHS community team co-located with CAMHS, children's disability social care, adult ID services and paediatrics, with add-on PBS team, crisis, IHTT, respite and local inpatient unit. Although, bringing all of these services would likely bring its own challenges. Overall, we would advocate for an ID CAMHS team, either within or alongside a CAMHS team, rather than a fully integrated one-size-fits-all CAMHS team. Some of the other disadvantages can be mitigated by good working relationships with education, parent support groups, CYP advocacy and all other involved parties. It is important to consider the wider multiagency and financial context in service design and clear remit, service level agreements and commissioning.

What should ID CAMHS deliver?

First, it is important to consider what our aims are and what are we trying to achieve. There is perhaps a general consensus that we are trying to reduce behaviours that challenge, increase mental and emotional well-being, and psychologically support families and young people. When we think about how we might achieve this, the task is potentially quite large. In order to affect change, we need to work with the individual, the family, across environments and systems and with other professionals.

Positive Behaviour Support (PBS) is now relatively well established and an adopted framework within intellectual disability services. We will not go over the literature here, nor provide in depth discussions. In brief, PBS uses a multi-element approach aimed at increasing quality of life and decreasing behaviours that challenge and reduce restrictive practice. '*PBS means that people receive the right support at the right time. The right conditions need to be created and maintained so people can achieve the quality of life that they want and deserve to have. Successful implementation needs a whole organisation approach and ongoing commitment*' (BILD CAPBS, 2016). A PBS Competence Framework has been developed by The PBS Academy (2015). We will use this framework in the table below to map what ID CAMHS should provide at the different levels.

Table 11.3: The PBS Competence Framework

Different ways in which PBS may be implemented	Examples of what ID CAMHS might offer
Single practitioner co-ordinating all elements of the framework and leading each stage for the process on a case-by-case basis.	Assessments, formulations and interventions for challenging behaviours.
	Interventions may be wide ranging from supporting skill development in the young person, to adapted CBT, to making adjustments with the environment to supporting language development, to family work, to pharmacological intervention.
	Consideration of any health issues that may impact upon the young person.
	Consideration of communication or sensory needs where there are possible links with challenging behaviours.
	Psychiatric or cognitive assessment that contributes to PBS plan.
	Psychoeducation on specific aspects.
	Linking in and sharing PBS plans with the other relevant agencies involved in the young person's care.
In team partnerships between a range of professionals and a person's regular carers.	Leaders meeting and linking in, forming partnerships in their approach to care provided, particularly in relation to:
	Special Schools: having a named link worker or some system of regular connection, consultations, bespoke training.
	Paediatricians: joint clinics between psychiatrist and paediatrician for more complex cases.
	Disabled children's social work teams: regularly discussing and reviewing young people.
	Forming links with other relevant agencies in the area e.g. understanding of roles and referral systems, offering training and consultations.
	Mainstream CAMHS teams who might be working with mild ID through consultations, training and some joint working.
	Short-term break providers/multi-agency teams: consultation/bespoke training to local services.

Different ways in which PBS may be implemented	Examples of what ID CAMHS might offer
Through system-wide approaches whereby the PBS framework is implemented at varying levels or tiers of intensity across an entire organisation (such as schools, residential or small group homes, or specialist inpatient settings) or geographical territory.	Members of steering groups for different agendas e.g. STOMP/STAMP, Special Educational Needs and disability local disability groups, Transforming Care Partnership, where key leaders of provider services and commissioners may meet. Training programme for professionals and carers on PBS and different specific topics related to ID and behaviours that challenge.

(**Positive Behaviour Support Academy, 2015**)

Staff composition and skill set for CAMHS for children and young people with ID

Staff composition

It is important to have the right skill set within a team and the right number of professionals in order to deliver the service intended. There are several influences on the numbers of staff required in any service, including such factors as:

- the type of service provision, including the aims and what the service specification includes
- the geography/accessibility
- amount of black and ethnic minority groups
- any local culture issues.

When considering the staffing needs of this population there are other influencing factors; it is not just a case of simply seeing what the guidance is for other CAMHS teams, because the ID population is different. For ID CAMHS:

- In general terms, there are more professionals involved with a young person as the severity of disability increases. This means that at a service level there are potentially more people to liaise with and the greater the importance of working system-wide becomes.

- The young person is more likely to be more dependent upon the carers in their different environment, so more engagement and liaison is required to support assessments, formulations and interventions at an individual level.

- More complex health needs are more likely, so again more liaison work, and assessments may take longer.

- Work with families can take longer due to a process of adjustment that many families go through.

- Increased levels of poverty (Emerson & Hatton, 2007).

- A critical mass is needed to cover annual leave, sickness and continuing professional development, in order to maintain the appropriate skill mix.

- Perhaps most importantly, in a large review of the mental health needs of young people intellectual disabilities, Emerson & Hatton (2007) found that they were six times more likely to have a diagnosable psychiatric disorder than their non-learning disabled peers.

There have been several attempts by the Royal College of Psychiatrists to specify staffing for services that include mild, moderate and severe ID. The latest is the CR200 (2016), which states that a community team per 100,000 population should have 5-6 wtes (whole time equivalents). It further suggests that in a typical population of 250,000 for significant disabilities (we have taken this to mean moderate, severe and profound intellectual disabilities, IQ<50) there should be: 1.0 wte consultant psychiatrist; 2.0 wte clinical psychologists; 5.0 wte intellectual disability nurses; 2.0 wte support workers; 1.0 wte speech and language therapist; 1.0 wte occupational therapist.

We would agree with this in principle, and probably highlight that this is quite generous from our own experiences. However, rather than being prescriptive of the number of wtes for each professional group, there should be some flexibility depending upon the skill set of those in the post and further training undertaken. Professional mixes may change overtime. For example, assessments of sensory needs as part of a wider assessment of challenging behaviour are appropriate and everyone should have baseline training in areas such as the function of challenging behaviours, communication needs, health issues to be aware of etc. In addition to this, for some professions such as consultant psychiatrists where recruitment can be a challenge owing to national shortages, a 1.0 wte may be needed in order to attract a person into post.

We would therefore propose a flexible approach and for a 250,000 population that a 9.0 wte staffing is needed, with a range of 7.2-11.0 wtes. The higher the range, the more that will be achievable within any given service specification. See Table 11.4 for the wte range, depending upon the skill set.

Table 11.4: Wte ranges

Staffing	WTE Range
Consultant Psychiatrist	0.7-1.0*
Clinical Psychologists	2-3
Support Workers	1.5-2
Intellectual Disability Nurses	2-3
Speech & Language Therapist	0.5-1.0
Occupational Therapist	0.5-1.0
TOTAL	7.2-11

Skill sets

There are several publications that address the skill sets required for an ID CAMHS in more detail. The CR200 (2016) by the Royal College of Psychiatrists describes in depth psychiatric services for young people with ID; *A Toolkit for Clinicians* (2009) by Emerson & Hatton outlines the roles of those professionals involved, and Rossiter and Armstrong (2015) outlined what 'good' looks like for psychological services for children and young people with ID and their families. Currently a big influence on our services and the skill sets required are Positive Behaviour Principles and, of course, the STOMP/STAMP campaign. The next section will look in more depth about how a service might work and the function of the team, but to help frame this the skill sets needed for an ID CAMHS should include:

- Essential core skills.
- Psychiatry assessment and intervention.
- Mental health assessments and knowledge of co-morbidities.
- Health issues, diagnostic over-shadowing.
- Positive behaviour support approaches.
- Complex formulations and intervention.
- Skill development: relaxation, sexuality and puberty knowledge, emotional regulation.
- Cognitive assessments and formulations.
- Communication assessments.
- Sensory assessments.

- Family work and psychoeducation.

- Training and consultation.

- Family therapy.

- Knowledge and expertise in trauma.

- Knowledge and expertise in attachment difficulties.

- Adapted psychotherapies e.g. Cognitive Behaviour Therapy.

- Sleep assessment and intervention.

- More specific health knowledge in specialist areas e.g. epilepsy, continence, eating difficulties.

The importance of leadership and team culture

Literature about the function and way in which ID CAMHS works is relatively sparse compared to other mental health service provision, and is often made up of either descriptions of models or aspirational commissioning (CR200, 2016; Emerson & Hatton, 2009; Rossiter & Armstrong, 2015). Different models of service have already been described above but it is important to consider what is provided. By this we mean what the service actually delivers, how it works and what its aims are. Another essential ingredient to all of this, which we will briefly address, is leadership and team culture.

'It aint what you do, it's the way that you do it' was not only a top selling 80s pop song by Fun Boy Three & Bananarama, it taps into a really important concept and principle. In the NHS, 'values' has become a central driver with six values that form part of the NHS Constitution. Having a strong value base is central to many theories and models of leadership. While we strongly believe that leadership and culture are always extremely important in any organisation, we would argue that it is particularly important for ID CAMHS, and hence want to highlight this. A review of leadership models in the NHS is beyond the scope of this chapter, however the Healthcare Leadership Model (NHS Leadership Academy, 2013) provides a useful framework. Its nine dimensions reference many of the important aspects that are crucial for what ID CAMHS should be delivering. This is mapped out below.

Table 11.5: Healthcare Leadership Model

Dimension of Leadership	Importance for ID CAMHS
Leading with Care	The families we work with are often experiencing strong, ongoing emotions and it is therefore really important that we care for our team members to help them deliver a great service and manage strong emotions. Young people with ID are often stigmatised, so additional advocacy may be needed.
Engaging the Team	Teamwork is essential for ID CAMHS, with much autonomous and community work. The team is contributing to a lot of different levels of the system around the young person to support mental health care. Staff engagement is therefore important with all contributions being valued.
Sharing the Vision	Having clear aims and inspiring hope for our teams and families is essential, given the ongoing nature of the challenges that young people and families will experience. The team needs to be optimistic, responsive to needs, and convey hope.
Influencing for Results	We need to work across many organisations, and so collaborative working to influence positive outcomes is essential. We need to sensitively negotiate on shared outcomes and resources in order to influence change together.
Evaluating Information	Important for all areas of the NHS, evaluating information is key to both the individual care in carrying out functional analysis to working systemically and helping to develop strong evidence bases. Given the limited services for ID CAMHS we need to think and look broadly for models of care and ways to deliver high level of performance and creatively manage resources.
Inspiring a Shared Purpose	This is important for all NHS services to 'create a shared purpose for diverse individuals doing different work'. Families need to have hope, and in order to support PBS plans we need to negotiate a shared purpose with families, young people and often schools and other key people involved.
Holding to Account	Like all areas of the NHS, having clear expectations about what success looks like is really important, especially for autonomous working. As we may often have to advocate for young people with an ID and their families, we need to be prepared to hold others and ourselves to account.

Dimension of Leadership	Importance for ID CAMHS
Connecting our Service	The outcomes for the young people we work with are dependent upon all the services working together. The Positive Behaviour Support Academy (2015) explains that one of three ways that PBS may be implemented is through a system-wide approach. Understanding the culture, structure and demands on our different agencies is crucial in helping us to connect and negotiate individual goals and service-wide approaches.
Developing Capability	With a limited workforce in intellectual disability services, it is essential that we develop capability in our teams. While having clear roles is always essential, there needs to be some flexibility with a limited workforce as well as the opportunity to develop staff.

(NHS Leadership Academy, 2013)

The Centre for the Advancement of Positive Behaviour Support's Practice Paper 3 highlights the importance of the leadership role in ID services. *'Leaders have to employ a range of emotional and interpersonal skills to develop a culture and values that reinforce positive practice in a process of winning hearts and minds'* (BILD CAPBS, 2015). The paper refers to the importance of the practice of frontline managers and the concept of 'Practice Leadership', outlining some specific approaches including:

- knowing what's going on
- developing staff practice for PBS and reducing restrictive practice
- managing staff/service user (rapport, relationship and emotional experiences)
- shaping staff practice
- external organisations e.g. employers and regulatory agencies
- personal characteristics and actions of successful leaders.

In summary, attending to our leadership and team culture in ID-CAMHS is just as important as the staff composition and skill set required.

Conclusion

To meet the mental health and behaviour needs of children and young people with moderate, severe and profound intellectual disabilities, services need to have the right commissioned staffing numbers and service structures, with appropriate specialist skills and knowledge that will then lead to a reasonably adjusted, equitable provision of care with a rights based, compassionate ethos. Service providers should work with commissioners to jointly learn about the needs of this population. Without all of these factors being comprehensively met in a meaningful way, there will be unmet needs among this group and services functioning sub-optimally under pressure. This will lead to poor quality of life and further high costs to the individual and society over time. Dame Christine Lenehan's quote in *These Are Our Children* (2017) is pertinent here: *'The failure to deliver appropriate care and support is not to do with activity, or interest or commitment but to do with not giving the necessary outcomes for this group of children'.*

References

Department of Health (2012) *Transforming care: A national response to Winterbourne View Hospital.* DoH.

Department of Health and Social Care and Department for Education (2017) *Transforming children and young people's mental health provision: a green paper.* DoH.

Emerson E & Hatton C (2007) *The Mental Health of Children and Adolescents with Intellectual disabilities in Britain.* Lancaster University.

Lenehan C (2017a) *These Are Our Children.* Council for Disabled Children.

Lenehan C (2017b) 'Good Intentions, Good Enough?' The Lenehan Review into Residential Special Schools. Council for Disabled Children.

Narey M (2016) *Residential Care in England* [online]. Department for Education. Available at: www.gov.uk/government/publications/childrens-residential-care-in-england (accessed June 2020).

NHS (2018) *Children and Young People Transforming Care Workforce (CYP TCW) – Report and Recommendations.*

NHS (2019) *The NHS Long Term Plan* [online]. Available at: www.longtermplan.nhs.uk (accessed June 2020).

NHS England (2019) *STOMP-STAMP pledge resources* [online]. Available at: www.england.nhs.uk/publication/stomp-stamp-pledge-resources/ (accessed June 2020).

Positive Behaviour Support Academy (2015) *Positive Behaviour Support Competence Framework* [online]. Available at: www.pbsacademy.org.uk/pbs-competence-framework/ (accessed June 2020).

Reid C, Sholl C & Gore N (2013) seeking to prevent residential care for young people with intellectual disabilities and challenging behaviour: examples and early outcomes from the Ealing ITSBS. *Tizard Learning Disability Review.*

CR200 (2016) *Psychiatric services for young people with intellectual disabilities.* Royal College of Psychiatrists.

Bernard S &Turk J (2009) *Developing Mental Health Services for Children and Adolescents with Intellectual disabilities: A Toolkit for Clinicians.* The Royal College of Psychiatrists.

Rossiter R & Armstrong H (2015) *Delivering psychological services for children and young people with intellectual disabilities and their families.* The British Psychological Society.

British Institute of Intellectual disabilities, Centre for the Advancement of Positive Behaviour Support (2016) *The five signs of good PBS* [online]. Available at: www.bild.org.uk/capbs/pbsinformation/ (accessed June 2020).

Chapter 12: Transition into adult life

Eddie Chaplin, Jane McCarthy and Dr Sarah H Bernard

Chapter summary

The chapter provides an understanding of the key issues for practitioners to consider in supporting a young person with intellectual disability transitioning into adult life. It highlights the relevance of key national policy to the process of transition and gives examples of good and poor transition, along with the importance of including the young person's family or carer in transition planning. What good practice looks like is explored, ensuring that those involved in transition planning are working alongside the young person early on to achieve a successful outcome for the individual as they move into adulthood.

Introduction

Significant failings in the way the NHS and social care services support children with intellectual disability have been reported (Hardy *et al*, 2017; Lenahan, 2017). The transition into adulthood is a greater problem for young people with an intellectual disability, particularly when transitioning into adult services (Hudson, 2003). Transition planning, as we know it today, originates from the Education Act (1994) and associated Code of Practice (Department for Education and Skills, 2001). and subsequent revision (Department for Education and Department of Health, 2015). However, over 20 years later it is still the case that all too often young people experience a disconnect with services at the transition stage, often due to poor cohesion. There are a number of reasons as to why this might be, including: different age limits adopted by services, a lack of planning and referral processes, and a lack of local services, which often means levels of support received as a young person are decreased or do not exist (Hudson, 2006). Such transitions are complex and there is often a poor understanding of the process from those involved including the person, family, carers and service providers.

Transition is an anxiety provoking time for the young adult, as it is for family, carers and specialist support staff. Young people with an intellectual disability in transitioning to adulthood are often a) socially marginalised, b) more dependent on family, and c) have fewer education and work options (Forte *et al*, 2011). The aims of the transition process are to ensure a smooth transfer from children's to adult services and to provide opportunities for the young person that allows personal achievement and growth. The transition to adult life can be difficult, but it can also be an opportunity for growing as a person, starting new relationships and developing greater opportunities for independence. The majority of young people with intellectual disability will continue to live at home and may not have the same opportunities for social activities, independence, freedom of choice over their day-to-day lives as others. In addition, they will not have the same opportunities for employment and to achieve financial independence.

Young people with an intellectual disability transitioning into adulthood are less likely to attend post-secondary education, live independently, or see friends at least weekly in the early years after leaving school (Newman *et al*, 2010). A study looking at what predicts good outcomes for young people post-school (Papay, 2011) found that the involvement of the young person improved outcomes in terms of taking up post-secondary education, being employed and more likely to see friends. Family involvement was also a good prediction of post-secondary education and the young person reporting enjoying life two to four years after leaving high school. Work experience seemed to be predicted in the long-term by life skills instructions. Parental expectation was a strong predictor of future employment, post-secondary education. Although there are a number of barriers, it is the role of services to ensure that there is a personalised, family-centred care package that anticipate future support needs for the young person's well-being, both immediate and in the long term, whether this is educational, vocational physical or psychological. To do this requires a life-course approach and joining up of services between agencies to work towards easing the different transition stages during childhood into adult services.

Policy

The Department of Health (DH) (2008) guide on improving transitions for young people with long-term conditions defines the transition process as:

'...*a purposeful, planned process that addresses the medical, psychological and educational/vocational needs of adolescents and young people with chronic physical or medical conditions as they move from child-centred to adult-centred health care systems*' (p14).

The current systems and the 2008 guide to transition from the DH are built on the 2001 White Paper *Valuing People* (DH, 2001), which proposed care models to ensure a workforce and wider skilled community-based service provision to meet the needs of young people with intellectual disability. This commitment was reiterated in *Valuing People Now* (DH, 2009), which came two years after *Aiming High for Disabled Children: Better Support for Families* (HM Treasury, 2007), which outlined how local areas would be supported to improve transition arrangements using and improving upon person-centred approaches to improve support, quality and capacity. Although policy and guidance has set out a clear vision of what services should look like, in reality there is great disparity in how regions have interpreted and implemented that vision.

Another factor that influences implementation is whether compliance with policy is mandatory or not. Not all policy has been implemented as anticipated. The Transforming Care programme, which came about following wide scale abuse of people with intellectual disability at Winterbourne View, aimed to improve the lives of children, young people and adults with an intellectual disability and associated conditions. The aim of Transforming Care was to move 3,250 children and adults in assessment and treatment units back to their local communities by 1st June 2014 (Bubb, 2014). Failing to do this has illustrated the crisis that transition services are in with the number of children who are in-patients having doubled (Norman Lamb 'Future of the Transforming Care programme', debated in Parliament 5 July 2018). This situation is further exacerbated by a lack of appropriate and quality services such as those outlined in the Mansell Reports (DH, 1993; 2007), which emphasise the following key points:

- It is the responsibility of commissioners to ensure that services meet the needs of individuals, their families and carers.
- There is a focus on personalisation and prevention in social care.
- Commissioners should ensure services can deliver a high level of support and care to people with complex needs/challenging behaviour.
- Services and support should be provided locally where possible.

(DH, 2012, Annex A, p50)

Achieving independence

The definition of successful adult life transition includes independent living, achieving employment and developing interpersonal and intimate relationships. The professions most able to support people with intellectual disability may to some extent vary depending on the networks already known to the person. In some countries this may be a family physician, such as in Canada, where specialist intellectual disability services are not widely available and this will be the best option (Ally *et al*, 2018). For this to happen, transition planning should map all of the systems encountered by the young person with intellectual disability, ensuring that areas of strength are identified to assist the transition process, while those aspects where more support is required should be prioritised for intervention (Small *et al*, 2013). For young people with intellectual disability, the transition to adulthood will bring additional challenges as their experiences will often differ from those of young people without intellectual disability. For example, for many young adults with intellectual disability, major decision making is more likely to be undertaken by parents and carers for longer than if they lived independently. For others without capacity and who are less able, decision making is often taken from them at an earlier age, albeit with input from those trying to understand what the young person would choose in given situations. Having choices about managing finances, leaving home, going to work and what to do in their social life, should be part of normal transition. For those in residential or hospital placements, independence may be more difficult to achieve as the young person is not exposed to situations to develop life skills.

Carer's perspective

The impact of transition on the parents of young people with complex health needs can be huge. It can be a particularly difficult time because of changes such as puberty occurring as part of the journey into adulthood. In a study in which carers were asked about their experiences of being involved, they reported that they felt that the system works against them. Carers often felt that it was assumed and expected by services and clinicians that they would readily adapt to changing circumstances, with neither support nor understanding from services as to how it would affect and impact upon them and their families. Rather than being engaged, carers felt they were not used or used inappropriately by services and, even worse, were not informed, with experiences of services neither answering nor returning phone calls (Emery *et al*, 2013). Given these issues, carers will often try to make local arrangements in the absence of support e.g. home schooling where there is little or no local specialist provision. This may often unintentionally widen the gulf between families and services, but it is seen as the only solution available to ensure their child or young person continues to receive an education.

Transition and mental health

The chances of a more successful transition into adult life may be affected by additional health problems such as mental illness, challenging behaviour and epilepsy, which will affect the person's ability to achieve independence and leave home. Recent research indicates that, along with limited adaptive behaviour, impaired language development and low socio-economic status, poor socialisation is a major risk factor for psychiatric disturbance in children with intellectual disabilities.

Young people who have mental health problems and severe intellectual disabilities also fall through the gap in terms of accessing services. This occurrence has been described as a 'white hole', as many young people are not being picked up by any services. Young adults with intellectual disability and psychiatric disorders diagnosed in childhood may not have received specialist mental health services as children and adolescents. School would be a useful setting to make contacts with mental health specialist services in order to identify mental health problems before transition and the requirement for proactive treatment. Young people with other types of neurodevelopmental disorders, such as those with autism and attention deficit hyperactive disorder, have been found to have significant needs during transition (Murphy *et al*, 2018). Commonly, their health needs are undiagnosed even when in contact with clinical services. Upon transition into adult life, their contact with treatment and support services actually reduces rather than increases. This is further evidence of how services need to be much more proactive in responding to the complexity of young people with intellectual disability.

The recent *National Health Service* model 'Building the right support' (2015) outlines a model for people with intellectual disability who have significant behavioural and mental health needs. This model includes that each person should have:

- A good and meaningful everyday life, which includes education, employment and social activities.
- That there is person-centred planning that is proactive.
- The person should have choice and control over their health and care.
- The person should be supported to live in the community.
- The person should have choices over their housing.

Meaningful activities and support in the community after leaving full time education are extremely important factors in helping young people with mental health needs fulfil their aspirations. For those with mental health needs, a model of care is required that either operates as a transition team or through shared protocols to ensure effective transition between adolescent and adult mental health services, recognising that this transition does not always need to occur at the age of 18 years. Systems approaches such as these, however, still rely heavily on individual clinicians being proactive and supporting transition in the young person's interest (Ally *et al*, 2018).

Case vignettes

Many people wrongly assume that the aim of transition is to plan services, but it's much more than that. It is about planning lives and futures for both the young person and their circle of support. It is a time when the young person can voice their aspirations and ambitions, when they can map out a pathway to their future.

The earlier this process starts the better chance it will have of working. How does the young person see themselves in the wider world? What does independence look like to them? What support do they require with housing and employment choices?

Figure 12.1: An example of poor and good transition

Poor transition	Good transition
John is 24 and has severe intellectual disability with problems relating to self-harm and aggression towards others. He currently receives support led by children's services and lives in a residential college. Since his teens, it has been clear that there is a lack of willingness from adult services to take over, although there are specific adult services that are commissioned for some specialist care. With no joined up working and a lack of local services, there is no individualised person-centred plan for the future or any transition pathway documents relating to John's needs. Due to an impasse over the transition and support of John, who has just received a notice to quit college as he will soon be too old, adult services request a Mental Health Act assessment following which John is detained in hospital for a period for assessment. In hospital and unable to grasp what is going on around him, John's behaviour deteriorates and questions are raised about his mental health. He is subject to a treatment order.	Chantelle has a mild intellectual disability, an enlarged heart and cerebral palsy. When just 13, she was encouraged by her family to think about her future. This included talking about what support, and in what form, she might require in the future as she became more independent and less reliant on others. Chantelle, along with two other friends from her school, have expressed a wish to live together when they are 'grown up'. To make sure everyone knows, Chantelle and her family write a transition pathway document, which will also let people know about Chantelle's likes and dislikes and let everyone know who is doing what to support her. For example, Chantelle's head teacher is responsible for sending out invites for her transition meetings. At the age of 19, Chantelle got her wish to live with her school friends in supported living accommodation. Although the team and Chantelle's circle of support are different, with creative commissioning, a joint funded, continuing care package was developed that supports her to attend a college course on working with animals. Chantelle also works one afternoon a week at a local vet thanks to the support of her transition plan. Those supporting Chantelle are also aware of what to do and who does what if she is in need of urgent physical care. This assessment and joint working includes associated risks with support plans related to her cerebral palsy, such as seizures or problems related to her heart.

Best practice in transition and implications for practice

There are many opinions as to what makes or contributes to a positive experience during transition (see Figure 12.2). For transition planning to work, all the systems encountered by the young person need to be identified and mapped to ensure that they are not being failed (Small *et al*, 2013). This requires partnership working in order to determine processes and protocols that need to be in place. Transition protocols vary widely in practice, but it is essential to include the needs and wishes of the young person in their transition planning, and to ensure that services are tailored towards achieving positive outcomes (Kaehne & Beyer, 2014).

Figure 12.2: Good practice in transitioning services

Heslop *et al*, 2002	Deb *et al*, 2006	Viner, 2008	Barron *et al*, 2014
a) Co-ordination: inter-agency working. b) Comprehensive and effective transition plan for all young people. c) Continuity of key workers; a seamless transition from children's to adult services. d) Choice: more and better involvement of young people and their families in the transition process. e) Communication between agencies, and between agencies and families. f) Independent advocacy for young people.	a) Transition planning. b) Transition co-ordination, use of a transition co-ordinator. c) Service user involvement. d) Needs assessment. e) Identify needs of clients, incorporate the views of carers and the other professional bodies. f) Use of health action plans and person-centred planning.	a) Preparing the young person and their families for transition. b) Preparing the adult services. c) Listening to the needs of young people.	a) Good information transfer across teams (information continuity). b) A period of parallel care/joint working between teams (relational continuity). c) Adequate transition planning (cross-boundary and team continuity). d) Continuity of care following transition (long-term continuity).

A major implication for practice is the need to put in place appropriate and useful transition planning processes that consider the young people's views and aspirations. Friendships are very important, and ways of maintaining these after transition are to be supported through involving the young person in activities and leisure pursuits in their local community. Many young people lose their social networks as a result of the transition from school to college. Young people with intellectual disability should have more opportunities to be involved in mainstream activities and to engage with peers in their local communities.

Conclusion

The key issue in planning for transition into an adult life for people with intellectual disability is that we need to be proactive, engaging the young person and/or their family in developing transition plans. There needs to be clarity as to what the young person considers to be a successful outcome. Transition planning should respect the autonomy of the young person with intellectual disability if they are to achieve a successful and positive move into adult life. We need to take into account their personal needs such as their life skills, social skills and where they are developmentally in regards to emotional, social and communication needs. As practitioners, we must advocate for transition planning early on in the adolescent years, allowing sufficient preparation time to work in partnership with the young person and their family and wider support systems.

Key Learning Points

- Transition planning needs to start early and involve the young person from the beginning of the process.
- The family and carers must be involved in the transition process.
- There should be local planning for shared protocols or teams that focus on the transition process specifically for those young people with behavioural and mental health needs.

References

Ally, S., Boyd, K., Abells, D., Amaria, K., Hamdani, Y., Loh, A., Niel, U., Sacks, S., Shea, S., Sullivan, W.F. and Hennen, B., 2018. Improving transition to adulthood for adolescents with intellectual and developmental disabilities: Proactive developmental and systems perspective. *Canadian Family Physician*, 64(Suppl 2), pp.S37-S43.

Barron AD, Coyle D, Paliokosta E & Hassiotis A (2014) *Transition for Children with Intellectual Disabilities [online]. University of Hertfordshire.* Available at: www.intellectualdisability.info/life-stages/articles/transition-for-children-with-intellectual-disabilities (accessed June 2020).

Bubb S (2014) Winterbourne View: Time for Change Transforming the commissioning of services for people with intellectual disabilities and/or autism, A report by the Transforming Care and Commissioning Steering Group, chaired by Sir Stephen Bubb – 2014

Building the Right Support: A national plan to develop community services and close inpatient facilities for people with a learning disability and/or autism who display behaviours that challenge, including those with a mental health condition. October 2015, NHS England. www.england.nhs.uk

Deb S, LeMesurier N & Bathia N (2006) *Guidelines for services for young people (14-25 years) with learning difficulties/ disabilities and mental health problems/ challenging behaviours: Quick Reference Guide (QRG).* University of Birmingham, Birmingham, UK.

Department for Education and Department of Health (2015) *Special educational needs and disability code of practice: 0 to 25 years* [online]. Available at: www.gov.uk/government/publications/send-code-of-practice-0-to-25 (accessed June 2019).

Department of Health (1993) Services for People with Intellectual disabilities and Challenging Behaviour or Mental Health Needs. London, UK: The Stationery Office. The Mansell Report LSBU Research Report: December 2017 59.

Department of Health, (2001) *Valuing People: A New Strategy for Learning Disability for the 21st Century London.* The Stationery Office.

Department of Health (2007) *Services for people with intellectual disabilities and challenging behaviour or mental health needs (Revised Edition).* London, UK: The Stationery Office. The Mansell Report (revised).

Department of Health (2008) *Transition: Moving on well: A good practice guide for health professionals and their partners on transition planning for young people with complex health or disability.* London: Department of Health.

Department of Health (2009) *Valuing People Now: A New Three-Year Strategy for People with Intellectual disabilities.* London, UK: The Stationery Office.

Department of Health (2012) *Transforming Care: A national response to Winterbourne View Hospital: Review Final Report.* London, UK: The Stationery Office.

Department for Education and Skills (2001). *Special Educational Needs Code of Practice* DfES/581/2001

Emery H, Jones B & Chaplin E (2013) A comparison of carers needs for service users cared for both in and out of area. *Advances in Mental Health and Intellectual Disabilities* **7** (3) 143-151.

Forte M, Jahoda A & Dagnan D (2011) An anxious time? Exploring the nature of worries experienced by young people with a mild to moderate intellectual disability as they make the transition to adulthood. *British Journal of Clinical Psychology* **50** (4) 398–411.

Her Majesty's Treasury, (2007). Department for Education and Skills (2007) Aiming High for disabled children: better support for families. Her Majesty's Treasury, London.

Heslop P, Mallett R, Simons K & Ward L (2002) *Bridging the Divide at Transition: What happens for young people with learning difficulties and their families.* BILD, Kidderminster.

Hardy S, Chaplin E & Tolchard B (2017) A Workforce Development Project: Working with Children and Young People with Intellectual disabilities and Comorbid Mental Health/Autism/Challenging Behaviour Conditions – Commissioned by the Tavistock and Portman NHS Foundation Trust.

Hudson B (2003) From adolescence to young adulthood: the partnership challenge for learning disability services in England. *Disability & Society* **18** (3) 259–276.

Hudson B (2006) Making and missing connections: learning disability services and the transition from adolescence to adulthood. *Disability & Society* **21** (1) 47–60.

Kaehne A & Beyer S (2014) Person-centred reviews as a Mechanism for planning the post-school transition of young people with intellectual disability. *Journal of Intellectual Disability Research* **58** (7) 603–613.

Lenehan C (2017) These are our children: a review by Dame Christine Lenehan, Commissioned by the Department of Health.

Murphy D, Glaser K, Hayward H, Eklund H, Cadman T, Findon J, Woodhouse E, Ashwood K, Beecham J, Bolton P, McEwen F, Wilson E, Ecker C, Wong I, Simonoff E, Russell A, McCarthy J, Chaplin E, Young S & Asherson P (2018) *Crossing the Divide: Effective treatments for people with neurodevelopmental disorders across the lifespan and intellectual ability.* National Institute for Health Research Report, Grant Number RP-PG-0606-1045.

Newman L, Wagner M, Cameto R, Knokey A & Shaver D (2010) *Comparisons across time of the outcomes of youth with disabilities up to 4 years after high school. A report from the National Longitudinal Transition Study (NLTS) and the National Longitudinal Transition Study-2 (NLTS2)*. Menlo Park, CA: SRI International.

Papay CK (2011) *Best practices in transition to adult life for youth with intellectual disabilities: A national perspective using the national longitudinal transition study-2.*

Small N, Raghavan R & Pawson N (2013) An ecological approach to seeking and utilising the views of young people with intellectual disabilities in transition planning. *Journal of intellectual disabilities* **17** (4) 283–300.

Viner RM (2008) Transition of care from paediatric to adult services: one part of improved health services for adolescents. *Archives of Disease in Childhood* **93** (2) 160–163.

Other titles from Pavilion Publishing

Mental Health in Intellectual Disabilities (5th Edition)
Edited by Colin Hemmings

Now in its 5th edition, Mental Health in Intellectual Disabilities continues to address the need for a handbook which, while well-grounded in research and latest clinical practice, is essentially non-academic and accessible for staff occupying many roles. For example support workers and managers in learning disability service settings, GPs, psychologists, psychiatrists, community learning disability teams and other professionals who may find themselves supporting a person with an intellectual disability from time to time, as well as students of mental health and intellectual disability.

The 5th edition represents a complete revision and updating, aiming to address key knowledge requirements and concerns of people working in the field and provide opportunities for reflection and continuing professional development. The content is illustrated by case studies to help the reader explore how best to address mental health issues in practice.

A mental health assessment of children and adolescents across the full developmental spectrum
By Steve Moss

The Moss-PAS (ChA) is for mental health assessment of children and adolescents across the full developmental spectrum, including intellectual disability. Like the *MPAS-ID*, the *Moss-PAS (ChA)* uses a scoring system that provides a single score for each of the diagnostic constellations, each of the constellations having a corresponding threshold. If the child or young person reaches or exceeds the threshold it is probable that they warrant a diagnosis in that constellation. However, a strong emphasis is placed on the importance of expert clinical judgement when interpreting the scores in relation to other pieces of information, e.g. history, environment, and family factors.

The Moss-PAS (ChA) provides a semi-structured interview format in which the young person may contribute to whatever degree they are able, or it may be conducted by informant interview only. Question wordings, symptom definitions and glossary notes were developed by clinical experts from Canada and the UK. Updated from the original ChA-PAS Interview, all necessary symptoms for ICD 11 and DSM-5 diagnoses are included.

Person-centred Active Support training pack and self-study guide (2nd ed)

By Beadle-Brown, J., Murphy, B. and Bradshaw, J.

The principles of active support are based on a sound evidence base from behaviour and learning theory and are explored in Person-centred Active Support Training Pack (2nd Edition). And as such are what we know works best for everyone who needs support to be independent, exercise choice and control and be a contributing part of their local community.

This new training resource reflects the changes in the social care and learning disability context in the UK as well as in many other countries, and the valuable experience the authors have gained from 13 years of using the resources for training in many different settings.

This training pack comes with a copy of the fully revised, new edition of Person-centred Active Support self-study guide, including new video, which can also be purchased separately for self study.

The book is designed to provide the learner with knowledge about what active support is, why it is important, what it looks like in practice, and some of the key facts around what is needed for success.

The book is designed for people to follow as self-study or as part of a training programme. It includes videos and exercises to promote independent thinking and learning. It is available in hard copy and digital formats and provides about 5 to 7 hours of learning, with a certificate of completion.